MEAL PREP FOR TWO

MEAL PREP

for
TWO

8 Weekly Plans & 75 Recipes
to Get Healthier Together

CASEY SEIDEN, MS, RD, CDN, CDE

ROCKRIDGE
PRESS

To my husband, who inspires me daily,
and because I promised to always take care of you
and help you eat your vegetables.

Zesty Beef Meatballs with Bok Choy and Brown Rice, page 68

Contents

Introduction

Can you think of a time when preparing food was less stressful?

For me, life seemed easier when I was a young, single undergraduate student. I went to class and worked a few hours a week, and although I lived with roommates, my schedule and meals were my own. After finishing my studies, I landed a nutrition job in New York City, where I quickly met my future husband. Going from being an unattached student in the mountains to being in a relationship and working two jobs in a chaotic city was definitely a transition.

But one of the biggest changes during that time for both me and my partner was our eating habits. Restaurants were our date-night activity of choice, and small-apartment living didn't always inspire cooking meals together. On top of that, I was learning that the man I was falling in love with was not enamored with my way of eating. It turns out I was dating my toughest nutrition case study: a "selective" adult eater who disliked most vegetables and preferred that meals be a combination of meat, cheese, and carbs.

Although I wouldn't trade the meals we enjoyed while dating, my husband and I both look back with astonishment at the money spent, dishes turned down because one of us didn't like *that*, and general lack of attention to our overall nutrition. Luckily, as our relationship status changed from dating and living apart to married and creating a home together, our attention to our health—physically, emotionally, and mentally—graduated as well. Our kitchen became a learning lab, where new foods were introduced slowly, and dinners came together with less stress due to improved communication about meal prepping.

Getting into the habit of meal prep has changed our home for the better. Meal prepping has taught us not only about building simple and balanced meals but also about communication, patience, and the value of time spent together. Through meal prepping, we have prioritized our health in a way that is less stressful, without breaking the bank. As someone's partner and as a dietitian, I have learned that meal prep can be a tool for eating healthier—and it's really not as much work as you may think. If we can do it, so can you.

Just like a new relationship, meal prepping may not be smooth sailing at first, but I've designed this book to help you succeed. Even if you don't follow the same diet principles, you can adapt meals for your different tastes, diets, and portion size preferences. I will walk you through the stages of meal prep—from learning to get one meal for the week packed up to tackling a week's worth of dinners. Cooking and meal prep do not have to be complicated. Meals can be simple, nutritious, and completely delicious.

In writing this book, I wanted to create the ultimate resource for couples like me and my partner: busy people in a loving relationship who value their health and delicious food but want to avoid overspending or creating stress. In fact, I encourage any pair of two—those in a small household, friends living together— to use this book.

Whether you are just starting out or are simply looking for new recipes and kitchen inspiration, this book will give you the tools and resources to prep with ease so that you and your partner can eat healthier, spend less money, and enjoy more time outside the kitchen.

PART ONE

PREPPING
for
TWO

BEFORE WE DIVE INTO COOKING, let's get to know a little bit more about the fundamentals of meal prepping—specifically, how to meal prep for two people! I will walk you through the nuances of meal prepping for two and show you how doable it really is. You'll learn how it can advance your health goals, satisfy your taste preferences, and fit your budget. We will explore every couple's favorite place—the grocery store—and how to minimize your time and spending there. I also offer general tips for storage, food safety, and food serving.

Then, you'll be ready for showtime—eight weekly meal prep plans for two. Each plan has a theme to help make weekly meal decisions easy. To ease you into food prep, I've designed the plans to progress from simple to more complex, but each plan is delicious and easy to accomplish for a couple of new or experienced cooks in the kitchen. If you're a bit nervous to venture into meal prep, don't be. Grab your sous chef and apron up.

MEAL PREP 101

When I was a student studying to become a dietitian, I constructed dozens of meal plans. Every eating occasion was accounted for, calculated, and prescribed for someone else to follow. As I moved into clinical practice and began cooking for two, I quickly realized that meal plans were great for school assignments but not so practical for real life or relationships. From that moment on, I said goodbye to meal planning and welcomed meal prepping.

Meal prepping means scheduling time to prepare and cook several self-selected meals at once to be packed and eaten later. Prepping gives you flexibility; for example, Tuesday's lunch can become Thursday's dinner. Prepping as a duo can help you and your partner feel prepared for the week, allow you to spend more time together, and support you in getting healthier and feeling your best. The information in this section will equip you with the tools you need to get started.

MAKING IT DUO-ABLE

Sure, you probably already know meal prep is a great idea. But most of the plans and tips out there feature a plan for *me*, and you're likely thinking is this even possible for an *us*? Food prep for two people won't take much time or effort if you use this book. I will walk you through the tools and containers you'll want to have on hand (not as many as you think) and show you how to schedule your time in the kitchen so that you can efficiently prep meals and snacks to be enjoyed within one to five days.

Flexibility is yours with the tips and tools you'll find in this book. You and your partner will be able to eat the same or different food for each meal. I'll show you how to adapt portions for different appetites and how to accommodate different food preferences. Your confidence in meal prep will only continue to grow by practicing together. Meal prepping for two is absolutely duo-able!

BENEFITS OF PREPPING FOR TWO

Meal prepping for two can be beneficial for your health, your wallet, and your relationship. Here are five of the top benefits of meal prepping for two.

Get healthier together. Meal prep encourages you to be intentional about what you're eating and how much. Planning and portioning ahead of time will set you up for a successful week and curb impulsive food decisions at the store, while also allowing you to ask, "What sounds good to us?" Meal prepping will ensure that your meals are appropriately balanced, always including vegetables, whole grains, and an animal or easy plant protein option.

Maximize time and minimize stress. The last thing many couples want to do after a long day is wrangle the frustrating question, "So, what's for dinner?" Work is stressful enough. Completing some meal prep on a weekend or a night that is a little less busy can help maximize hang time together in the evenings or allow for a few extra minutes of sleep rather than a hurried morning without breakfast.

Spend less money. If you've ever gone grocery shopping and picked up a random mix of ingredients without a plan for them only to find they've gone bad and you have to toss them a week later, meal prepping is for you. By strategizing some meals and snacks, you'll be able to save money rather than pitch pricey produce. You'll also learn how to repurpose staple items, like herbs, yogurt, and other condiments, for later in the week to get the most bang for your buck.

Become better cooks. Meal prep is designed to be simple, so if you or your better half aren't quite master chefs yet, that's okay. Just by dedicating to cook more at home, you'll likely pick up some new knife skills, hone your kitchen smarts, and become better cooks together.

Communicate better. After mastering some of the plans in this book, you'll soon be on your own and coming up with your own meal prep schedules and plans, so communication about what dishes are going to be cooked, who will do the shopping, and when the meals will be eaten is critical. By prioritizing healthy eating through meal prep, your communication skills as a couple will grow leaps and bounds.

PREP IN FIVE STEPS

This book includes eight weekly meal prep plans for two people. Each plan tells you exactly what to purchase, how to manage your time in the kitchen, and how much to portion out.

After trying these plans out, you'll want to know how to start building your own meal prep plans. My best advice is to be patient and start small. If you aren't prepping at all right now, start by choosing one meal, maybe breakfast, and get that ready for five days of the week. As your confidence grows, add three days' worth of lunch prep, and so on. By following my Five Prep Steps, you'll be able to prep multiple meals and snacks for several days at a time.

When to Prep

Start by picking one or two days that work for you to prep. The preps in this book give you the option of cooking once or twice throughout the week. You may want to break up the work over two days, but if you're both up for it, all the steps can be done on one. In our house, Sunday afternoon has become prep time. Then, halfway through the week, as meals and pantry items have been depleted, we reassess, refresh, and cook small meals to finish the week. If one person in the partnership works an untraditional schedule with days off during the week, you may consider taking turns to coordinate prep. Meal prep has to work for both your schedules if you're going to succeed.

What to Prep

How do you decide which meals to prep? If your top consideration is simplicity and efficiency, look for recipes with five ingredients that can be cooked in one pan. If you are motivated by health considerations, select recipes that help treat

BUDGET HACKS

My partner and I consider ourselves foodies, but that doesn't mean we want to spend all our hard-earned money at the grocery store. Cooking at home is a great cost-cutting step that meal prepping will make even more effective.

Meal prep gently nudges you to look at your week's expenditures as a whole, which can help save money in the long run. Since my partner and I started buying a large amount of groceries, we've been able to identify items that go a long way and others that we could consider swapping out for a less expensive store brand. Having food ready to be eaten at home tamps down the impulse to order takeout or pick up pricy packaged snack foods. Best of all, as your weekday food costs decrease, your cash for weekend splurge meals or special occasions increases.

Need help cutting costs? Here are some tips:

Eat more plants. Meals can become more expensive if always planned around proteins like fresh meat and seafood. Canned varieties are less expensive, nonperishable, and time-saving. But you can save even more money by eating eggs, pulses (beans, peas, lentils), soy products, nuts, and seeds a few times per week. Eating plant-based protein is recommended for our health as well.

Balance convenience and saving. Grocers are catering to consumer demand for preprepped ingredients more than ever, but these ingredients often come at a price. For example, a chopped and bagged veggie slaw mix is super convenient, but it's more expensive than purchasing the individual ingredients. If you and your partner split the prepping task, the extra work might pay off in leftovers that can be repurposed. Find a financial and effort balance that works for you.

Buy from the bulk section. Self-serve sections of the supermarket are goldmines for saving cash. If recipes call for only a half cup of a specific nut, for example, stop by the bulk section and see if the unit price is less expensive than the price for the bagged version. For the same reasons, if you plan on making a lot of quinoa over the next month, the bulk section is usually a better deal and involves less packaging than the boxed products on the shelf.

Befriend the freezer section. Using less expensive frozen items can help with quick cooking and prep. For example, you could add a handful of frozen broccoli into your meal prep container of prepped protein and grain. By the next day's lunch, the broccoli will have thawed a bit and will complete its cooking when heated up with everything else. I go for fresh first, but if my option is purchasing a fresh vegetable that is out of season and costs more, I'm going to get my frozen veg on.

Order online. The ultimate hack to saving money and time these days seems to be ordering groceries online. Websites like FreshDirect, AmazonFresh, and Thrive Market make it easy for couples. Create a shared account and you can each add to the shopping cart. Not every online shopping portal will save you major money all the time, but again, it's worth balancing out the convenience with the cost.

or prevent a certain condition. When feeding only two people, the chance of having leftover ingredients and staple items is high, so perhaps your main priority is avoiding food waste by choosing recipes that allow you to use up those ingredients and items.

In part 2, you'll find additional breakfast, lunch/dinner, snack, and staple recipes to give you even more prep-friendly options, which you can mix and match in the outlined plans or use to construct your own plan. You can adapt these recipes to needs and tastes. For example, the Caribbean Stuffed Sweet Potatoes (page 132) can be topped with slow-cooked pork or made vegetarian with red beans. The Tuna Burger with Sun-Dried Tomato Tapenade (page 127) can be served in a pita pocket or wrapped in lettuce. For a partner with celiac disease or a gluten sensitivity, the Tex-Mex Tortilla Soup (page 126) can be topped with either flour or corn tortilla strips.

Food Shopping

After deciding what you're going to cook, check your kitchen and cross off items you already have. Next, make your list. I recommend shopping early morning on a weekend prep day or after the predinner rush if you're cooking during the week. Limit fresh produce, meat, seafood, and dairy to only the amounts specified in your prep; other grains and staple items may be bought in bulk. If your store has a self-serve section, stop there first so you can compare the unit price to the prepackaged price.

Prep and Cook

Efficient prep days lead to happy couples. For each meal prep plan, I have outlined a suggested flow of tasks. In general, a meal prep dance for two could look like this:

1   One person chops vegetables and breaks down proteins for the recipes that take the longest to prepare, such as soup, slow cooker, and roasting recipes. These longer meals should be started first if they're in your plan.

2   While one person chops, the other can prepare any sauces or seasonings. We love to use the All-Purpose Mediterranean Spice Blend (page 142) for roasting veggies, so my partner may measure and mix that up while I chop. As if by magic, the two recipe components come together just as the oven finishes preheating.

3 While one of you puts together no-cook recipes for breakfasts, such as the Tropical Chia Pudding (page 24), the other can prepare stovetop recipes, such as sautés or scrambles.

4 While one of you portions and packs cooked recipe components, the other can wash dishes.

Portion and Package

This last step in the prep process—portion and package—is something I want to specifically highlight. One of the benefits of meal prep is that a portioned amount of food is packed for easy accessibility. Portioning also helps us be more mindful of the amount of food we serve ourselves and eat.

The meal preps in this book provide portion recommendations for the average adult according to the *2015–2020 Dietary Guidelines for Americans* and USDA MyPlate. Generally, these meals provide an appropriate mix of foods and varied nutrients within an appropriate calorie level. They focus on making half your plate vegetables, a quarter grains, and a quarter lean protein; limiting saturated fats and added sugars; and including a serving of fruit or dairy. In my work as a dietitian, I prefer to keep the focus off exact calories and grams of macro- and micronutrients unless nutritionally and medically necessary; however, I do understand that many people appreciate knowing calories and estimated daily requirements. The following section provides a little more guidance on determining your individual energy needs, as well as ways to adjust portion sizes.

PREPPING WITH DIFFERENT NEEDS

There is no denying that my husband and I have different nutritional needs and preferences. Some days my appetite feels as though it can't be satisfied, and I eat double his serving. Other days, both of us enjoy smaller plates. He tolerates spicy foods a little bit less, whereas I love condiments and strong flavors.

Everyone has their own ever-shifting interests and preferences, but that doesn't mean meal prepping for two people isn't doable. I have designed these plans to cater to two average adults who are looking to prioritize a balanced eating pattern together. As differences inevitably arise, you may wish to consult some of the following tools and tips.

Ultimately, you know your household and partner the best, so you may have other priorities, but the two general areas I recommend figuring out with your partner are food differences (different intolerances, dietary guidelines, or preferences) and portion needs.

Food Differences

Here are some general guidelines for meal prepping to accommodate different food preferences or tolerances.

1. **Discuss your food intolerances.** A peanut allergy cannot be ignored, but something like one's spice tolerance is also good to keep in mind.
2. **Discuss your diet differences.** At some point you and your partner may prefer different foods. If one of you is following a vegetarian diet, brainstorm meal ideas that can easily swap out the animal protein for a protein that is plant based, such as beans or lentils.
3. **Identify what you both dislike.** Meal prepping allows you to avoid foods that one or both of you dislikes by using substitutes or convenient versions (i.e., frozen) to add to your helping.
4. **Identify what you both love.** I recommend making a "meals we love" sticky note as a reminder of home-run meal ideas.
5. **Determine whether routine or variety is most important.** Discuss with your partner what your meal needs are for the week and plan your week accordingly.

Portion Differences

Calories have become a feared word in today's diet culture, but it's important to remember that a calorie is simply a unit of energy that all foods, including fruits and vegetables, contain. Focusing on counting calories can be a source of stress for many people. As a dietitian promoting intuitive eating, and through my personal experience, I have found that living by a calorie limit is not sustainable. My husband and I both focus on nutrient-dense foods, use plates and bowls that accommodate reasonable portions, and tune in to our hunger and fullness. If we anticipate that one of us is going to be a bit hungrier, we may adjust recipes ahead of time or lean on our freezer stock to bulk up a dish. Nevertheless, hunger can be tough to anticipate, so we try to go with the flow and always have nutritious options on hand.

DIVIDE AND CONQUER

What can be accomplished by one can be completed by two in half the time! With a partner in the kitchen, prep work is easier and certainly faster than if one person were doing all of it alone. I recommend identifying each of your strengths and how much time you each have to help out. Here are some ways to make meal prepping as efficient as possible:

Collect recipes to try. My least favorite task is choosing the recipes to make, but my partner loves flipping through online cooking magazines and recipe blogs. We have learned to make a virtual recipe collection by screenshotting recipes we come across and saving them in a shared photo album. Then we scroll through our saved photos and choose recipes that sound good to prep that week.

Assess your kitchen stock. Having a cleaned-out pantry and refrigerator helps immensely. While one of you drafts the grocery list, another can be stationed at the refrigerator and freezer to check for items that you already have or that need to be tossed. It's also a good idea to assess your baking staples and spices. If you buy in bulk and store grains in glass jars, see if you can condense the leftover amount into a smaller jar to make more space.

Split up the groceries. If you're shopping together, each of you should have assigned sections of the store to collect the needed items. One person can zigzag the aisles while the other attacks the perimeter, and you can meet at the checkout. Alternatively, one of you can go to the store to pick up fresh items while the other person stays home and preps foods that you already have on hand.

Divvy up the cooking tasks. This is where knowing your strengths really comes in handy. The person who safely chops faster could be in charge of cutting the vegetables and proteins, while the other partner could start the actual cooking.

Pack and wash at once. While one person packs the prepped food, the other can scrub dishes. Cleaning as you go is also a good way to involve a partner who isn't big on cooking and ensure that you're not faced with a mountain of pots and pans at the end.

Everyone has a baseline calorie need for daily living based on age, sex, weight, height, and activity level. According to the *2015–2020 Dietary Guidelines for Americans*, a moderately active adult female and male need 1,600 to 2,000 and 2,200 to 2,600 calories per day, respectively. To find a more precise estimate of your calorie needs, you can use one of the USDA's online calculators.

This book's preps are developed with a focus on whole, unprocessed foods. The nutrition information is provided at the end of each recipe, but if you begin to consume plants in the form of vegetables and fruits, whole grains, legumes, seafood, lean meats, and low-fat dairy, your calorie intake should settle at an appropriate level that is sustainable for each of you.

STORAGE FOR TWO

The end goal of meal prep is grab-and-go food. Having containers and a good storage system is vital to your success. Storage may be an upfront cost, but think of your meal prep tools as investments in your health. Your container collection can start small. Note what you already have, consider repurposing condiment jars, and use the following guidelines to build your stock. I have a tiny New York City kitchen with about three cabinets, so I consider my storage containers carefully and appreciate having an organized pantry and refrigerator.

Containers

Storage containers need to keep your food fresh and protected from air exposure and contamination. They also need to accommodate the amount of food you will be portioning out for each of you, so I recommend getting a variety of sizes if you anticipate that your servings will differ greatly.

No matter which containers you choose, be sure to consider two important factors: (1) Are they leakproof? (2) Are they safe to be used in the microwave, freezer, and dishwasher? There are few things worse than opening your lunch bag to find its contents spilled, so make sure the container's seal is strong. If you're making the commitment to meal prepping for a healthier lifestyle, you want your containers to go the distance, so choose ones that hold up to heat and cold.

Again, your collection can start small. Limited storage may ultimately sway for how many days at a time you prep because you may need to wash prep containers midweek. For the simplest prep, let's say three days of breakfast and some snacks, you should have six single-serving storage containers as well as one larger one for the snack recipe. As work-friendly lunches are prepped, two more containers per day will be needed. You can pre-portion some dinners, which will require more containers, or store some recipes, such as a chili or soup, in one large container and reheat the portions in bowls.

These are some staple meal prep containers:

Single or multicompartment: My partner and I are big fans of mixing everything together, but not everyone likes their food touching. For us, the single compartment works well, but divided containers are great if you want to enjoy foods separately. You and your partner can get a mix of them to meet your needs.

Stackable/nestable: Having a tiny New York City kitchen has reinforced to me that containers need to fit neatly together for maximal space saving and organization. Even if your cabinet space is more generous, having containers that stack and nest makes them easy to find and keeps the kitchen tidy. Note that divided glass containers may not nest as nicely, but they are stackable with the lids attached.

Plastic: The pros of using plastic containers are that they are lightweight, stack neatly, and are convenient when commuting with your food. On the other hand, some plastic containers are still made with bisphenol A (BPA), a synthetic chemical that may be linked to harmful effects on the brain, blood pressure, and developing fetuses and newborns. Due to these concerns, look for the BPA-free sticker when purchasing plastic containers, and use plastic storage for cold items only.

Glass: For ultimate durability and reheating food, glass is best. A set of square, rectangular, or round glass containers is immensely helpful, and having mason jars for fun salad presentations or soups is a good idea as well. Some of these containers may not even need to be purchased. Wash out pasta sauce or jam jars to repurpose for storage. Glass may be more cumbersome to store, but I find the versatility and safety to be worth the space.

Eco-friendly bags: If you want to reduce plastic in your prep, shop for more eco-friendly storage bags. Available in varying sizes, bags from Stasher and (re)Zip have become my essentials for preserving food quality without taking up tons of space.

Labeling

Labeling containers is always a good idea for food safety, but especially when prepping for two people who may have different needs or tastes. No one wants to find chicken when they were expecting tofu or a sandwich with cheese if they're lactose intolerant. Along with each other's name, write the day you plan to eat that prep on the label. You could also consider assigning a different tape color for each person.

Thawing and Reheating

Once packaged, food should be stored for as long as indicated in the recipes. If you prep recipes from other cookbooks, be sure to follow general food storage safety guidelines as recommended by federal agencies. You can learn more at FoodSafety.gov.

The preps in this book are designed to generate refrigerator meals for the week, but some recipes are freezer friendly. Consider making double batches of some recipes, perhaps when you have extra time on a weekend prep day, to freeze and enjoy in the future.

It's important to reheat food properly to reduce your risk of foodborne illness. When microwaving, stir food halfway through to ensure even cooking. You may even want a thermometer handy to ensure the food reaches at least 165°F. If you remove containers from the freezer, never leave them on the countertop to thaw. Place the container in the refrigerator the night before, submerge it in cold water, or thaw the food in the microwave and cook it immediately.

What Not to Prep

Although you may feel yourself growing more confident and thinking you can prep and store everything, there is a limit. For example, sandwiches and wraps risk getting soggy if fully prepped with their fillings, especially if the filling is meant to be reheated. I recommend packing the bread on the side and assembling the finished wrap at mealtime. Also, if you're only going to prep on Sunday, consider that cooked chicken may not taste *exactly* the same by Friday, so you may want to plan a bean-based dish for the end of the week.

HOW TO STORE FOOD PROPERLY

Food safety is no laughing matter, and when you're cooking for two, that means even more food to be wary of. Here are some general food storage guidelines to keep in mind:

→ Refrigerate perishable foods within two hours, including cooked foods that have been packed and whole items post-shopping trip. In the summer, cut this time to one hour.

→ Avoid putting hot food straight into the refrigerator. To cool it more quickly, place it in shallow containers.

→ Pack the refrigerator with care, and avoid overstuffing for best air circulation.

Below is a chart spelling out storage times, according to the USDA.

FOOD	REFRIGERATOR	FREEZER
Salads: egg, chicken, ham, tuna, macaroni	3 to 5 days	Does not freeze well
Soups and stews: vegetable or meat based	3 to 4 days	2 to 3 months
Egg casseroles or bakes (cooked)	3 to 4 days	2 to 3 months
Leftovers: pizza, beans	3 to 4 days	1 to 2 months
Leftovers: cooked meat or poultry	3 to 4 days	2 to 6 months
Whole poultry (raw): chicken or turkey	1 to 2 days	1 year
Pieces of poultry (raw): chicken or turkey	1 to 2 days	9 months
Ground meats (raw): beef, turkey, veal, pork, lamb	1 to 2 days	3 to 4 months
Steaks (raw): beef, veal, lamb, pork	3 to 5 days	6 to 12 months
Chops (raw): beef, veal, lamb, pork	3 to 5 days	4 to 6 months

ABOUT THE MEAL PREP PLANS

This cookbook is the ultimate resource for meal prep plans for two people. Nobody is getting left behind! There are eight weeks of meal preps that include a mix of breakfasts, snacks, and lunches and dinners that can be used interchangeably. Here's a look at the preps:

	Breakfast	Lunch	Dinner	Snack
Meal Prep 1, page 19	2			1
Meal Prep 2, page 27	2	2		
Meal Prep 3, page 35			3	
Meal Prep 4, page 43			4	
Meal Prep 5, page 51			4	
Meal Prep 6, page 61	2	2		2
Meal Prep 7, page 73	2		5	
Meal Prep 8, page 89	2		5	

I'm a big fan of setting yourself up for success, which is why the meal prep described in this book progresses from easy to slightly more complex. Many people find breakfast to be a challenge when it comes to eating healthy, so I chose to ease you into prepping with some simple breakfast recipes. Snacks are often overlooked but can be an easy win for your health and wallet, so prepping bulk snacks is something I want you to get the hang of early on. Finally, the lunch and dinner recipes can be mixed and matched, so hot and cold main meal preps build in complexity throughout the plans. You do not have to tackle these preps in any particular order, but the first few are good ones to get your feet wet with together.

Every meal prep plan includes a shopping list for the week, the equipment and containers you'll need, and a recommended sequence of tasks to keep your prep day free of stress. Although I would be flattered if you cooked my plans over and over for months, I totally understand that people crave variety. For this reason, Part 2 includes extra recipes, which can be plugged into the existing plans or used to create your own prep plans.

Ready to prep? Let's go!

Tropical Chia Pudding,
page 24

PREP 1

START THE DAY TOGETHER

This first week of meal prep is all about making the transition as easy as possible by starting small and simple—and getting off to a good start in more than one way! A lot of people either overload on carbs at breakfast time or skip the meal entirely because they're rushing to get out the door. But this meal prep offers a solution for everyone: easy, portable breakfasts that are also nutritionally balanced in terms of carbohydrates, protein, and healthy fats. I personally love sneaking vegetables into breakfast—it's an easy win, especially when the vegetables are prepared in a tasty, flavorful way. Finally, a two-step, bulk snack recipe prevents midmorning or afternoon hangries. With this plan, both of you can start the day off right.

Day	Breakfast	Snack
M	Lazy Shakshuka	Coconut Cashew Energy Bites
T	Lazy Shakshuka	Coconut Cashew Energy Bites
W	Tropical Chia Pudding	Coconut Cashew Energy Bites
TH	Tropical Chia Pudding	Coconut Cashew Energy Bites
F	Tropical Chia Pudding	Coconut Cashew Energy Bites

SHOPPING LIST

Pantry

- ☐ Almond milk, plain unsweetened (24 ounces)
- ☐ Cashews, raw and unsalted (1 ½ cups)
- ☐ Chia seeds (4 tablespoons)
- ☐ Coconut, unsweetened shredded (¾ cups)
- ☐ Dates, pitted (1 cup)
- ☐ Dates, medjool (12 dates)
- ☐ Diced tomatoes, no-salt-added, 1 (14.5-ounce) can
- ☐ Oil, olive, extra-virgin
- ☐ Pita bread, whole-wheat, 2 (4-inch) rounds
- ☐ Vanilla extract

Herbs and Spices

- ☐ Cinnamon, ground
- ☐ Cumin, ground
- ☐ Garlic powder
- ☐ Red pepper flakes
- ☐ Salt
- ☐ Sea salt
- ☐ Sweet paprika

Produce

- ☐ Bell peppers, red (2)
- ☐ Kiwi fruit (6)
- ☐ Mangos, small (3)
- ☐ Onion, yellow (1)

Protein

- ☐ Eggs, large (4)

Dairy

- ☐ Feta cheese, crumbled (4 ounces)

EQUIPMENT

- ☐ Baking sheet
- ☐ Chef's knife
- ☐ Cutting board
- ☐ Food processor
- ☐ Measuring cups and spoons
- ☐ Mixing bowl
- ☐ Mixing spoon
- ☐ Sauce pots
- ☐ Skillet with lid

PREP CONTAINERS

- ☐ **Lazy Shakshuka:** 4 small glass containers, 4 small containers, 4 resealable sandwich bags (optional)
- ☐ **Tropical Chia Pudding:** 6 (16-ounce) mason jars with lids
- ☐ **Coconut Cashew Energy Bites:** 1 resealable gallon bag or medium container

STEP-BY-STEP PREP

Lazy Shakshuka, page 22	*Tropical Chia Pudding,* page 24	*Coconut Cashew Energy Bites,* page 25
► START HERE		
Prepare in full. ------▶	Prepare in full. ------▶	Prepare in full.

Lazy Shakshuka

NUT-FREE, VEGETARIAN

PREP 5 minutes • **COOK** 15 minutes • **MAKES** 4 servings

Wouldn't it be nice if your Monday breakfast was just as fancy as Sunday brunch out together? This luxurious shakshuka is kept "lazy" with jammy softboiled eggs rather than poached.

1 tablespoon extra-virgin olive oil

2 red bell peppers, chopped

1 medium yellow onion, sliced

1 (14.5-ounce) can diced tomatoes

1 teaspoon ground cumin

1 teaspoon sweet paprika

½ teaspoon garlic powder

½ teaspoon salt

Red pepper flakes

4 large eggs

1 cup crumbled feta cheese

2 (4-inch) whole-wheat pita bread rounds, cut into quarters

1. In a medium skillet, heat the olive oil over medium heat. When the oil is shimmering, add the bell peppers and onion. Sauté for about 5 minutes, until they start to soften.

2. Add the tomatoes and their juices, cumin, sweet paprika, garlic powder, and salt. Stir to combine and bring to a low simmer, then cover and cook for 10 minutes. Add red pepper flakes as desired. Set the skillet aside to cool.

3. While the pepper mixture is cooking, place the eggs in a large sauce pot and cover with water. Bring the water to a boil and then cover the pot and turn off the heat. After 6 minutes, drain the water and set the eggs in a bowl of ice water. Once cool, peel the eggs.

④ Into each of 4 glass containers, place a quarter of the tomato-pepper mixture and ¼ cup of crumbled feta. Set aside 2 quarters of pita bread and 1 egg to go with each container.

⑤ Store the airtight containers in the refrigerator for up to 4 days.

🔥 **Reheat** To reheat the pepper mixture, microwave uncovered for 1 to 2 minutes or return to a skillet to heat through. The softboiled egg can be mixed in afterward.

❄ **Freeze** The pepper mixture can be frozen for up to 3 months. To thaw, refrigerate overnight.

TIP The spice level of this recipe is easily customizable; simply add the red pepper flakes after dividing the mixture into two separate containers. Be sure to label them!

Per Serving (1 container): Calories: 315; Fat: 16g; Protein: 16g; Total Carbs: 31g; Fiber: 5g; Sodium: 856mg; Iron: 3mg

Tropical Chia Pudding

GLUTEN-FREE, VEGAN

PREP 10 minutes · **MAKES** 6 servings

Recipes that "cook" overnight are my jam, which is why I love chia pudding. The superfood seeds absorb up to 10 times their weight in water and are powerhouses of omega-3 fatty acids, protein, and soluble fiber.

Per container (×6)

- ½ cup plain unsweetened almond milk
- 2 tablespoons chia seeds
- ¼ teaspoon vanilla extract
- ¼ teaspoon ground cinnamon
- 1 kiwi fruit, peeled and chopped
- ½ cup chopped mango (3 cups total)
- 1 tablespoon unsweetened shredded coconut

1. Into each pint jar or other container, place the almond milk, chia seeds, vanilla, and cinnamon. Stir together or cover the jars with their lids and shake.

2. To each jar, add the kiwi, mango, and coconut.

3. Close with an airtight lid and store in the refrigerator for up to 5 days.

TIP If kiwi or mango aren't your tropical fruits of choice, feel free to change them out. Papaya, pineapple, guava, passion fruit, or dragon fruit would be excellent swaps. To save prep time, swap the fresh mango for frozen.

Per Serving (1 container): Calories: 298; Fat: 14g; Protein: 8g; Total Carbs: 38g; Fiber: 15g; Sodium: 189mg; Iron: 4mg

Coconut Cashew Energy Bites

GLUTEN-FREE, VEGAN

PREP 15 minutes · **MAKES** 10 bites

Energy bites are a great snack to have on hand for two busy people. These bites are easy to toss into your office or gym bag for an afternoon boost that won't weigh you down. If you're not a fan of munching on unsalted nuts, this recipe might help warm you up to the idea by combining protein-rich cashews and sweet dates.

1½ cups raw, unsalted cashews

1 cup pitted dates

¼ cup unsweetened shredded coconut

½ teaspoon sea salt

① In a food processor, process the cashews on high for about 3 minutes, until a coarse meal is formed.

② Add the dates, coconut, and salt, and process for about 5 minutes, or until the ingredients are finely chopped and start to come together.

③ With your hands, roll about 1 tablespoon of the mixture into a small ball. Repeat to use all the mixture. Set the balls on a baking sheet. Freeze for 10 to 15 minutes to set. Transfer the bites to a resealable bag.

④ Store in the refrigerator for up to 2 weeks.

❄ **Freeze** Freeze bites for up to 2 months.

TIP This is an easy recipe to double. If one of you tends to get hungrier, it's easy to grab an extra bite to pack with lunch or have after a workout.

Per Serving (1 bite): Calories: 191; Fat: 11g; Protein: 4g; Total Carbs: 20g; Fiber: 3g; Sodium: 98mg; Iron: 0mg

Loaded Lox Roll Ups,
page 32

PREP 2

WORKWEEK READY

One week of prep is under your belt—congratulations! This plan adds one more recipe, but your cooking time will remain minimal. This week, you can say goodbye to boring, unsatisfying work salads— this plan takes lunch to the next level. Making cold salads is a great way to start prepping for lunch because it requires no cook time. The breakfasts are also protein focused, so I recommend adding a piece of fruit in the mornings.

Day	Breakfast	Lunch
M	Swiss Chard and Feta Egg Muffins	Turkey Club Salad Jars
T	Swiss Chard and Feta Egg Muffins	Turkey Club Salad Jars
W	Loaded Lox Roll Ups	Tuna Salad–Stuffed Peppers
TH	Loaded Lox Roll Ups	Tuna Salad–Stuffed Peppers
F	Swiss Chard and Feta Egg Muffins	Turkey Club Salad Jars

SHOPPING LIST

Pantry

- ☐ Bread, sourdough, 6 (½-inch) slices
- ☐ Bread crumbs, panko (2 cups)
- ☐ Capers (¼ cup)
- ☐ Maple syrup
- ☐ Mustard, Dijon
- ☐ Nonstick olive oil cooking spray
- ☐ Oil, olive, extra-virgin
- ☐ Pumpkin seeds
- ☐ Tahini (6 ounces)
- ☐ Tortilla chips, corn (optional)
- ☐ Tortillas, whole-wheat, 4 (8-inch) rounds

Herbs and Spices

- ☐ Black peppercorns
- ☐ Chili powder
- ☐ Cumin, ground
- ☐ Red pepper flakes
- ☐ Salt
- ☐ Sea salt

Produce

- ☐ Avocado, large (1)
- ☐ Bell peppers, red (4)
- ☐ Cilantro, fresh (1 bunch)
- ☐ Garlic (2 cloves)
- ☐ Jalapeño pepper (1)
- ☐ Lemon (1)
- ☐ Lettuce, red leaf, large (2 heads)
- ☐ Lime (2)
- ☐ Red onion (1)
- ☐ Shallots (2)
- ☐ Swiss chard (1 bunch)
- ☐ Tomato, beefsteak (3)

Frozen

- ☐ Corn, 1 (10-ounce) bag

Protein

- ☐ Bacon (1 pound)
- ☐ Eggs, large (1 dozen)
- ☐ Lox or smoked salmon (1 pound)
- ☐ Tuna, albacore, water-packed, 2 (5-ounce) cans or pouches
- ☐ Turkey, boneless, skinless cutlets (1½ pounds)

Dairy

- ☐ Cream cheese (4 ounces)
- ☐ Feta cheese, crumbled (2 ounces)

EQUIPMENT

- ☐ Aluminum foil
- ☐ Baking sheets
- ☐ Chef's knife
- ☐ Cutting board
- ☐ Measuring cups and spoons
- ☐ Mixing bowls
- ☐ Muffin tin, 12-cup
- ☐ Paper towels
- ☐ Plate
- ☐ Skillet
- ☐ Whisk

PREP CONTAINERS

- ☐ **Turkey Club Salad Jars:** 6 quart-size mason jars with lids
- ☐ **Swiss Chard and Feta Egg Muffins:** 6 small containers
- ☐ **Loaded Lox Roll Ups:** plastic wrap or 4 eco-friendly bags
- ☐ **Tuna Salad–Stuffed Peppers:** 4 small containers and 4 small bags (optional)

STEP-BY-STEP PREP

Turkey Club Salad Jars, page 30	*Swiss Chard and Feta Egg Muffins,* page 31	*Loaded Lox Roll Ups,* page 32	*Tuna Salad–Stuffed Peppers,* page 33

► **START HERE**

Prepare steps ① through ②. While the bacon is baking . . .

Prepare steps ② through ⑦. While the egg muffins are baking . . .

Finish steps ③ through ⑤. While the egg muffins are cooling . . .

Prepare in full.

Finish step ⑧.

Prepare in full.

Turkey Club Salad Jars

DAIRY-FREE, NUT-FREE

PREP 10 minutes • COOK 15 minutes • MAKES 6 servings

This recipe doesn't make you choose between a salad or sandwich for lunch—it combines the best of both worlds! Using wide-mouth quart mason jars also means that you don't have to choose between eating a soggy salad or toting an extra dressing container around. This salad is layered so that the turkey marinates in the dressing to create a delicious, perfectly on-the-go lunch!

Per jar (×6)

2 strips bacon (12 total)

Nonstick olive oil cooking spray

1 (4-ounce) boneless, skinless turkey cutlet (1½ pounds total)

Pinch freshly ground black pepper

1 (½-inch) sourdough bread slice

2 tablespoons Dijon Tahini Dressing (page 143)

½ beefsteak tomato, chopped (3 tomatoes total)

2 packed cups torn red leaf lettuce (2 heads)

1. Preheat the oven to 375°F.

2. Line a baking sheet with aluminum foil and place on it 12 strips of bacon in a single layer. Cook for 15 to 20 minutes, until crispy. Transfer it to a plate lined with paper towels. Let drain, then roughly chop the bacon.

3. While the bacon is cooking, heat a large skillet over medium heat and lightly coat with cooking spray. Season the turkey cutlets on both sides with pepper. Cook for 3 to 4 minutes on each side, until the turkey has reached an internal temperature of 165°F. Repeat with any remaining cutlets as needed. Cut the turkey into 1-inch square pieces.

4. Toast the sourdough bread slices, then cut them into 1-inch cubes. While the bread is toasting, make the Dijon Tahini Dressing.

5. Into each quart-size jar, layer the dressing, chopped turkey cutlet, chopped tomato, toasted bread cubes, and torn lettuce. Store in the refrigerator for up to 5 days.

Serve Turn the jar upside down and shake, then dump the contents into a bowl and toss with a fork.

TIP Romaine or Bibb lettuce would also work well, or you may want to try kale for a unique spin.

Per Serving (1 container): Calories: 750; Fat: 46g; Protein: 54g; Total Carbs: 27g; Fiber: 2g; Sodium: 2013mg; Iron: 17mg

Swiss Chard and Feta Egg Muffins

GLUTEN-FREE OPTION, NUT-FREE, VEGETARIAN

PREP 10 minutes · **COOK** 30 minutes · **MAKES** 12 muffins

Say goodbye to fast-food egg muffins. These muffins are convenient, tasty, and healthy. For a veggie-phobic partner, these cups are a great way to introduce a new green food!

Nonstick olive oil
  cooking spray

12 large eggs

½ teaspoon salt

1 tablespoon extra-virgin
  olive oil, plus 2 teaspoons

2 shallots, minced

2 garlic cloves, minced

1 teaspoon red pepper flakes

4 cups chopped Swiss chard,
  ribs removed

⅓ cup crumbled feta cheese

2 tablespoons panko
  bread crumbs
  (or gluten-free)

1. Preheat the oven to 375°F.

2. Prepare a 12-muffin tin by spraying it lightly with cooking spray. Set aside.

3. In a medium bowl, whisk the eggs and salt. Set aside.

4. In a medium skillet, heat 1 tablespoon of olive oil over medium heat. When the oil is shimmering, add the shallots, garlic, and red pepper flakes. Cook for 3 to 4 minutes. Add the Swiss chard and sauté for 5 minutes, until the greens are just wilted. Turn off the heat.

5. Divide the chard mixture evenly into each muffin cup. Evenly pour the egg mixture over the vegetables to fill each cup. Distribute the feta evenly on top of each cup.

6. In a small bowl, combine the bread crumbs and the remaining 2 teaspoons of olive oil. Sprinkle this mixture evenly on top of each cup.

7. Bake for 20 minutes, until the tops are slightly browned and an inserted toothpick comes out clean.

8. Once cool, place 2 muffins into each of 6 airtight containers. Store in the refrigerator for up to 1 week.

Reheat Microwave for 1 to 2 minutes or reheat in a 375°F oven for 10 minutes.

Freeze Freeze muffins for up to 2 months. To thaw, refrigerate overnight.

Per Serving (2 muffins): Calories: 209; Fat: 14g; Protein: 14g; Total Carbs: 8g; Fiber: 1g; Sodium: 433mg; Iron: 3mg

Loaded Lox Roll Ups

NUT-FREE

PREP 10 minutes · **MAKES** 4 servings

As a native New Yorker, my husband loves bagels and lox, and as a dietitian, I'm on board for salmon's high omega-3 fatty acids and protein. These loaded lox roll ups can be stored in plastic wrap or bags and stacked on top of one another, so they take up very little space in the refrigerator.

4 (8-inch) whole-wheat tortillas

4 ounces cream cheese

1 pound lox or smoked salmon

¼ red onion, thinly sliced

¼ cup capers

1. On a clean surface or cutting board, lay a single tortilla. Spread a thin layer of cream cheese on it as a base. Layer 4 ounces of lox, a few red onion slices, and about 1 tablespoon of capers on the tortilla. Roll up the tortilla lengthwise.

2. Repeat this process with the remaining tortillas.

3. Wrap the rollups in plastic wrap or place in a food storage bag. Store in the refrigerator for up to 4 days.

TIP Cucumbers would be another great, crunchy addition to these wraps.

Per Serving (1 wrap): Calories: 356; Fat: 22g; Protein: 31g; Total Carbs: 15g; Fiber: 8g; Sodium: 2607mg; Iron: 1mg

Tuna Salad–Stuffed Peppers

DAIRY-FREE, GLUTEN-FREE, NUT-FREE

PREP 20 minutes · MAKES 4 servings

My husband isn't the only one in our relationship who won't eat certain foods. I hated canned tuna fish for years. However, we made a resolution to eat seafood twice per week, so I set out to find ways to enjoy canned tuna because it's portable and inexpensive. A tip for sustainable shopping—when buying canned fish, always look for white tuna that is pole or line caught.

2 (5-ounce) cans white albacore tuna

1 cup corn, fresh or frozen and thawed

1 avocado, peeled and pitted

⅓ cup chopped red onion

¼ cup chopped fresh cilantro

1 jalapeño pepper, seeded and finely diced

Juice of 2 limes

1 teaspoon ground cumin

1 teaspoon chili powder

½ teaspoon salt

¼ cup pumpkin seeds

4 small red bell peppers, seeded and cut in half lengthwise

Corn tortilla chips (optional)

① In a large bowl, using a fork, combine the tuna, corn, avocado, red onion, cilantro, jalapeño, lime juice, cumin, chili powder, and salt. Smash the avocado so that it binds all the ingredients together.

② Mix in the pumpkin seeds and if needed, adjust the seasoning to taste. Spoon equal parts of the mixture into each pepper half.

③ Place 2 stuffed pepper halves into each of 4 airtight containers. Store in the refrigerator for up to 4 days.

Serve If desired, serve with a handful of tortilla chips—just store these in separate bags or containers.

TIP This tuna salad takes on a Mexican flavor profile, but you can make it Greek-style by using add-ins like kalamata olives, pine nuts, feta, and lemon.

Per Serving (2 stuffed pepper halves): Calories: 286; Fat: 13g; Protein: 25g; Total Carbs: 25g; Fiber: 7g; Sodium: 337mg; Iron: 4mg

Creamy Peanut Noodles with Shrimp, page 39

PREP 3

BETTER THAN TAKEOUT

We all love having a date night every once in a while. Sometimes there's nothing better than you and yours curling up on the couch with some takeout, a bottle of wine, and a bingeworthy streaming show. But takeout can weigh heavily on your wallet (and perhaps even your waistline). That's why this week's meals are all about making takeout healthy and affordable. This week you'll even use up an entire head of red cabbage, an item that can be a challenge in terms of leftovers.

Day	Dinner
M	Caramelized Fennel and Ground Turkey Naan Pizzas
T	Creamy Peanut Noodles with Shrimp
W	Salsa Verde Veggie Enchilada Bake
TH	Creamy Peanut Noodles with Shrimp
F	Salsa Verde Veggie Enchilada Bake

SHOPPING LIST

Pantry

- [ ] Black beans, low-sodium, 1 (14.5-ounce) can
- [ ] Naan, plain or garlic (2 flatbreads)
- [ ] Oil, avocado
- [ ] Oil, olive, extra-virgin
- [ ] Oil, sesame
- [ ] Peanuts, unsalted (1 cup)
- [ ] Peanut butter
- [ ] Salsa verde, 1 (16-ounce) jar
- [ ] Soba noodles, 1 (10-ounce) package
- [ ] Soy sauce, low-sodium
- [ ] Sriracha
- [ ] Tortillas, corn, 8 (6-inch) rounds

Herbs and Spices

- [ ] Cumin, ground
- [ ] Red pepper flakes

Produce

- [ ] Carrot, large (1)
- [ ] Cilantro (1 bunch)
- [ ] Fennel bulbs (2)
- [ ] Garlic (3 cloves)
- [ ] Lime (1)
- [ ] Onion, red (1)
- [ ] Onion, yellow (1)
- [ ] Red cabbage, medium (1 head)
- [ ] Snow peas (⅓ pound)
- [ ] Zucchini (1 large)

Protein

- [ ] Shrimp, medium (1 pound)
- [ ] Turkey breast, ground (8 ounces)

Dairy

- [ ] Monterey cheese (8 ounces)
- [ ] Mozzarella, fresh (3 ounces)

EQUIPMENT

- [ ] Baking dish (9-by-7-inch)
- [ ] Baking sheet (optional)
- [ ] Blender (optional)
- [ ] Bowl, large
- [ ] Chef's knife
- [ ] Cutting board
- [ ] Grater/shredder
- [ ] Measuring cups and spoons
- [ ] Mixing spoons
- [ ] Sauce pots
- [ ] Skillet
- [ ] Spatula
- [ ] Strainer
- [ ] Tongs

PREP CONTAINERS

- [ ] **Salsa Verde Veggie Enchilada Bake:** 4 glass containers
- [ ] **Creamy Peanut Noodles with Shrimp:** 4 containers (glass optional)
- [ ] **Caramelized Fennel and Ground Turkey Naan Pizzas:** 2 glass containers

STEP-BY-STEP PREP

Salsa Verde Veggie Enchilada Bake, page 38	*Creamy Peanut Noodles with Shrimp,* page 39	*Caramelized Fennel and Ground Turkey Naan Pizzas,* page 40

▶ **START HERE**

Prepare through step ④.
While the enchiladas are baking... - - - - - - - - - - ⟶

Prepare in full.

Finish step ⑤. ◀ - - - - - - - - - - - - - - -

- ⟶ Prepare in full.

Salsa Verde Veggie Enchilada Bake

GLUTEN-FREE, NUT-FREE, VEGETARIAN

PREP 10 minutes · **COOK** 40 minutes · **MAKES** 4 servings

You can easily make your own flavorful and nutritious Mexican food for a fraction of the cost. Plus, casserole-type meals hold up really well in the refrigerator. This vegetarian option is nice on the wallet, but you can easily swap the beans for chicken or roasted pork.

1 tablespoon extra-virgin olive oil

1 yellow onion, chopped

1 zucchini, chopped (about 2 cups)

2 cups shredded red cabbage

1 (14.5-ounce) can low-sodium black beans, drained and rinsed

1 teaspoon ground cumin

2 cups jarred salsa verde, divided

8 (6-inch) corn tortillas

2 cups shredded Monterey cheese

¼ cup lightly packed fresh cilantro, roughly chopped

1. Preheat the oven to 350°F.

2. In a large skillet, heat the olive oil over medium heat. When the oil is shimmering, add the onion and sauté for 5 minutes, stirring occasionally. Add the zucchini and cabbage and sauté for 5 minutes. Add the black beans and cumin and stir to combine. Remove from the heat.

3. In a 9-by-7-inch baking dish, spread ½ cup of salsa verde in the bottom in an even, thin layer. Arrange 4 tortillas over the sauce, followed by the bean mix. Spoon another ½ cup of salsa over this vegetable layer. Place the remaining 4 tortillas on top and cover with the remaining 1 cup of salsa verde. Sprinkle the cheese over the top evenly.

4. Bake for 30 minutes until the edges are bubbly and the cheese just begins to brown. Remove from the oven and top with the cilantro. Slice into 4 even portions.

5. Into each of 4 containers, place 1 portion of enchilada bake. Store in the refrigerator for up to 5 days.

🔥 **Reheat** Reheat in the microwave for 1 to 2 minutes or in a 350°F oven for 15 minutes.

❄ **Freeze** Freeze for up to 2 months. To thaw, refrigerate overnight.

TIP Using a premade salsa saves time, but for a homemade recipe, see my quick and easy version of Salsa Verde (page 145).

Per Serving (1 container): Calories: 496; Fat: 22g; Protein: 23g; Total Carbs: 51g; Fiber: 8g; Sodium: 1917mg; Iron: 5mg

Creamy Peanut Noodles with Shrimp

DAIRY-FREE

PREP 20 minutes · **COOK** 10 minutes · **MAKES** 4 servings

If your partner isn't into shrimp, you can easily substitute grilled chicken or edamame. Peanut sauce makes anything taste amazing. Thai food is one of our favorite takeout cuisines to recreate at home. If one of you has a peanut allergy, you can make this sauce with sunflower seed butter. Eat this dish hot or cold.

1 cup Peanut Sauce for Everything (page 148)

10 ounces soba noodles

1 tablespoon avocado oil

1 pound medium shrimp, peeled, deveined, and tails removed

2 cups finely shredded red cabbage

2 cups halved snow peas

1 large carrot, shredded or cut into thin matchsticks

¼ cup unsalted peanuts, roughly chopped

½ cup chopped fresh cilantro

1. Make the Peanut Sauce for Everything and set aside.

2. Bring a large pot of water to a boil and cook the soba noodles according to the package instructions. Drain, rinse, and set aside in a large bowl.

3. In a medium skillet, heat the avocado oil over medium heat. When the oil is shimmering, cook the shrimp for 3 minutes, until starting to turn pink. Flip the shrimp and cook for another 3 minutes until opaque and slightly browned. Remove from the heat.

4. To the bowl with the noodles, add the cooked shrimp, red cabbage, snow peas, and carrot. Drizzle the peanut sauce over everything and, using tongs, toss to coat well. To finish, add the chopped peanuts and cilantro.

5. Into each of 4 containers, divide equal amounts of the noodle mixture. Store in the refrigerator for up to 4 days.

Reheat Warm in the microwave for 1 to 2 minutes or in a skillet over medium heat.

TIP If you're not planning on making the Salsa Verde Veggie Enchilada Bake this week, save yourself some time and purchase preshredded cabbage. Alternatively, shred an entire head of cabbage at once and freeze what you don't use for this recipe.

Per Serving (1 container): Calories: 585; Fat: 20g; Protein: 44g; Total Carbs: 66g; Fiber: 5g; Sodium: 1368mg; Iron: 9mg

Caramelized Fennel and Ground Turkey Naan Pizzas

NUT-FREE

PREP 5 minutes · COOK 20 minutes · MAKES 2 pizzas

Naan is a great "pizza" base; it's pre-portioned already, which means each person can customize their own toppings, and you can avoid unruly leftovers!

1 tablespoon extra-virgin olive oil

2 small fennel bulbs, fronds removed, halved, and thinly sliced

¼ red onion, sliced

3 garlic cloves, minced

8 ounces ground turkey breast

½ teaspoon red pepper flakes

2 naan flatbreads

3 ounces mozzarella cheese, torn

(1) Preheat the oven's broiler and set a rack about 6 inches from the heat source.

(2) In a medium skillet, heat the olive oil over medium heat. When the oil is shimmering, add the fennel, red onion, and garlic. Cook, stirring occasionally, until the mixture begins to brown. Add a small splash of water and cover the pan with a lid. Lower the heat and cook for 5 to 8 minutes. Uncover, stir the mixture, and cook for another 2 minutes. Transfer the mixture to a bowl and set aside.

(3) Return the skillet to medium heat and add the ground turkey and red pepper flakes. Using a spoon, break the meat up into crumbles. Cook until no more pink remains, about 5 minutes. Turn off the heat. Return the cooked fennel mixture to the skillet and combine.

(4) Using tongs or a large spoon, place even amounts of the turkey and fennel mixture onto each naan. Spread the mixture with the spoon or your hands to create an even layer. Divide the torn mozzarella between the 2 pizzas.

⑤ Place the pizzas under the broiler and cook for 5 to 7 minutes, until the bread crisps and the cheese browns. Remove from the oven and cut each pizza into 4 pieces.

⑥ Into each of 2 containers, place 4 slices of pizza. If you need to layer the slices, use pieces of wax or parchment paper in between. Store in the refrigerator for up to 3 days.

🔥 **Reheat** To reheat, microwave for 1 to 2 minutes or heat in an oven at 375°F for about 10 minutes.

❄️ **Freeze** Freeze for up to 2 months. To thaw, refrigerate overnight.

Per Serving (1 pizza): Calories: 664; Fat: 25g; Protein: 51g; Total Carbs: 57g; Fiber: 9g; Sodium: 444mg; Iron: 3mg

Slow Cooker Lentil Tagine, page 46

PREP 4

MEDITERRANEAN STAYCATION

Deep blue seas, salty breezes, the warm sun—and let's not forget about the beautiful, abundant produce! The Mediterranean diet is one of the best for weight loss, heart and brain health, cancer prevention, and diabetes prevention and control. If you and yours are longing to feel like you're on vacation—without feeling like your diet has gone on vacation, too—this week's meals are for you. The recipes in this plan ensure that you consume the recommended two servings of seafood per week, and they emphasize beans, legumes, and poultry. I recommend enjoying these meals with a glass of red wine!

Day	Lunch	Dinner
M	*Greek Turkey Burgers*	*Sheet Pan Ratatouille with Roasted Salmon*
T	*Sheet Pan Ratatouille with Roasted Salmon*	*Slow Cooker Lentil Tagine*
W	*Greek Turkey Burgers*	*Spring Panzanella*
TH	*Slow Cooker Lentil Tagine*	*Spring Panzanella*
F	*Spring Panzanella*	*Slow Cooker Lentil Tagine*

SHOPPING LIST

Pantry

- ☐ Almonds, raw unsalted (4 cups)
- ☐ Artichokes, 1 (14-ounce) can
- ☐ Bread, sourdough, 6 (½-inch) slices
- ☐ Chickpeas, low-sodium, 2 (15.5-ounce) cans
- ☐ Diced tomatoes, 1 (14.5-ounce) can
- ☐ Lentils, green or brown
- ☐ Nonstick olive oil cooking spray
- ☐ Oil, olive, extra-virgin
- ☐ Pita bread, whole-wheat, 2 (4-inch) rounds (optional)
- ☐ Sun-dried tomatoes, oil-packed or dried (1 ⅓ ounces or ⅔ ounces)
- ☐ Vegetable broth, low-sodium (48 ounces)
- ☐ Vinegar, red wine

Herbs and Spices

- ☐ Cinnamon, ground
- ☐ Coriander, ground
- ☐ Cumin, ground
- ☐ Garlic powder
- ☐ Oregano, dried
- ☐ Paprika
- ☐ Rosemary, dried
- ☐ Salt
- ☐ Sea salt
- ☐ Thyme, dried

Produce

- ☐ Carrots, medium (3)
- ☐ Cilantro (1 bunch)
- ☐ Eggplant, Italian (1)
- ☐ Garlic (1 head)
- ☐ Kale, curly (1 bunch)
- ☐ Onion, red (1)
- ☐ Onion, sweet (1)
- ☐ Onion, yellow (1)
- ☐ Potatoes, yellow, waxy (1 pound)
- ☐ Sugar snap peas (1 pound)
- ☐ Summer squash, yellow, medium (2)
- ☐ Tomatoes (5)
- ☐ Tomatoes, cherry (1 pint)
- ☐ Zucchini, medium (2)

Protein

- ☐ Ground turkey (1 pound)
- ☐ Salmon, 4 (4-ounce) fillets

Dairy

- ☐ Feta cheese, crumbled (4 ounces)
- ☐ Yogurt, plain (8 ounces) (optional)

EQUIPMENT

- ☐ Cast iron skillet (or grill)
- ☐ Chef's knife
- ☐ Cutting board
- ☐ Measuring cups and spoons
- ☐ Mixing bowl
- ☐ Mixing spoon
- ☐ Sheet pans
- ☐ Skillet with lid
- ☐ Slow cooker
- ☐ Whisk

PREP CONTAINERS

- [ ] **Slow Cooker Lentil Tagine:** 6 medium glass containers
- [ ] **Spring Panzanella:** 6 medium containers, 6 small containers (optional), 6 resealable sandwich bags (optional)
- [ ] **Sheet Pan Ratatouille with Roasted Salmon:** 4 medium glass containers
- [ ] **Greek Turkey Burgers:** 4 small containers and 4 resealable sandwich bags or plastic wrap (optional)

STEP-BY-STEP PREP

Spring Panzanella, page 47	*Slow Cooker Lentil Tagine,* page 46	*Sheet Pan Ratatouille with Roasted Salmon,* page 48	*Greek Turkey Burgers,* page 49

▶ **START HERE**

Preheat the oven to 350°F. ┈┈┈┈┈▶

Prepare step ①. While the stew cooks . . .

Prepare step ②. ◀┈┈┈┈┈ While the bread cubes bake . . . ┈┈┈┈┈▶

Prepare steps ② through ③. Raise the oven temperature to 450°F, then proceed with step ④. While the vegetables are roasting . . .

Finish steps ③ through ⑥. ◀┈┈┈┈┈

Finish steps ⑤ through ⑦. ┈┈▶

Prepare in full.

Finish steps ② through ④. ◀┈┈┈┈┈

Slow Cooker Lentil Tagine

DAIRY-FREE OPTION, GLUTEN-FREE, NUT-FREE, VEGETARIAN

PREP 15 minutes · COOK 2 to 3 hours · MAKES 6 servings

Busy weeks can easily be saved by a slow cooker meal for two. Dump in your ingredients, busy yourself with other tasks, and soon the house will smell amazing. This recipe is a riff on a Moroccan tagine, and the spices can be customized. Harissa or ras el hanout, if you can find them, would be excellent and authentic ways to spice up this dish.

1 pound yellow waxy potatoes, cut into ½-inch pieces

3 carrots, halved lengthwise and cut into ½-inch pieces

1½ cups green or brown lentils

1 (14.5-ounce) can diced tomatoes

1 yellow onion, chopped

3 garlic cloves, minced

3 teaspoons paprika

1½ teaspoons ground cumin

1½ teaspoons ground coriander

1½ teaspoons salt

¾ teaspoon ground cinnamon

6 cups low-sodium vegetable broth

1 cup chopped fresh cilantro

1 cup plain yogurt, for serving (optional)

1. In a slow cooker, combine the potatoes, carrots, lentils, tomatoes and their juices, onion, garlic, paprika, cumin, coriander, salt, and cinnamon. Pour in the vegetable broth to cover everything. Stir to combine. Cover and cook on high for 2 to 3 hours.

2. After about 1 hour, taste and adjust the seasoning to your liking and add extra liquid (vegetable broth or water) if you prefer a thinner stew.

3. At the end of the cooking time, into each of 6 containers, ladle a 1½ cup portion of stew and top with a sprinkle of fresh cilantro and a spoonful of yogurt (if using).

4. Store the airtight containers in the refrigerator for up to 5 days.

Reheat To reheat, microwave for 1 to 2 minutes.

Freeze Store in freezer-safe containers for up to 4 months. To thaw, refrigerate overnight.

TIP Lentils, unlike other beans and legumes, do not need to be soaked for 24 hours before cooking—they are speedy enough to cook straight from the bag or after being soaked for a mere 2 hours.

Per Serving (1 container): Calories: 268; Fat: 1g; Protein: 16g; Total Carbs: 48g; Fiber: 9g; Sodium: 695mg; Iron: 2mg

Spring Panzanella

DAIRY-FREE, VEGETARIAN

PREP 20 minutes · **COOK** 20 minutes · **MAKES** 6 servings

Panzanella is a rustic Tuscan bread salad that is tossed in juicy tomatoes and a bright vinegar dressing. Typically, panzanellas use day-old bread, which you can use if you prefer, but this recipe speeds up the process with oven toasting of the bread. The trick to making panzanella is deciding when to add the dressing. Pack the components separately and combine them right before eating, or allow the dressing and tomato juices to soften the bread for 1 to 2 days.

For the salad

8 cups sourdough bread, cut into 1-inch cubes

2 tablespoons extra-virgin olive oil

5 cups sugar snap peas, cut in half

5 medium tomatoes, roughly chopped

½ red onion, thinly sliced

1 (14-ounce) can artichokes, drained

2 (15-ounce) cans low-sodium chickpeas, drained and rinsed

1 cup almonds, roughly chopped

For the dressing

¼ cup extra-virgin olive oil

2 tablespoons red wine vinegar

1 teaspoon dried oregano

2 garlic cloves, minced

Pinch salt

① Preheat the oven to 350°F.

② Spread the bread cubes in an even layer on a sheet pan and toss them with the olive oil. Bake for 15 to 20 minutes until toasted. Set the cubes aside to cool.

③ In a large bowl, combine the snap peas, tomatoes, red onion, artichokes, chickpeas, and almonds.

④ To make the dressing, in a small bowl, whisk the olive oil, red wine vinegar, oregano, garlic, and salt.

⑤ Into each of 6 medium containers, place equal amounts of vegetable mix and bread cubes. Divide the dressing into 6 small containers and keep in the medium containers.

⑥ Store the airtight containers in the refrigerator for up to 5 days.

TIP Canned, frozen, or fresh artichoke hearts can be used in this salad.

Per Serving (1 container with dressing): Calories: 541; Fat: 25g; Protein: 18g; Total Carbs: 67g; Fiber: 15g; Sodium: 690mg; Iron: 6mg

Sheet Pan Ratatouille with Roasted Salmon

DAIRY-FREE, GLUTEN-FREE, NUT-FREE

PREP 15 minutes · **COOK** 50 minutes · **MAKES** 4 servings

A sheet pan makes meal prep for two supremely easy. This French-inspired ratatouille uses summer vegetables, but you can add anything you and your partner like. Be sure not to overcrowd the sheet pans—you don't want the vegetables to steam and get soggy!

1 tablespoon All-Purpose Mediterranean Spice Blend (page 142), divided

2 zucchini, halved lengthwise and cut into ½-inch-thick slices

2 yellow summer squash, halved lengthwise and cut into ½-inch-thick slices

2 cups chopped Italian eggplant

1 medium sweet onion, halved and cut into ¼-inch-thick slices

1 cup halved cherry tomatoes

3 tablespoons extra-virgin olive oil

4 (4-ounce) salmon fillets

Nonstick olive oil cooking spray

1. Preheat the oven to 450°F.

2. Make the All-Purpose Mediterranean Spice Blend.

3. In a large bowl, combine the zucchini, yellow squash, eggplant, onion, and tomatoes. Add the olive oil and 2 teaspoons of Spice Blend. Toss to combine. Pour the vegetables onto 2 sheet pans.

4. Roast for 30 to 40 minutes, turning with a spoon and rotating the pans halfway through, until the vegetables are tender and beginning to brown.

5. While the vegetables are roasting, prepare the salmon fillets by lightly spraying them with olive oil and sprinkling them with 1 teaspoon of the spice blend. Place the salmon in a cast iron skillet or baking dish that is broiler-safe and set aside.

6. Once the vegetables have finished roasting, set the oven to broil and place the salmon fillets on the center rack for 8 to 10 minutes, until lightly browned.

7. Into each of 4 containers, place a salmon fillet and equal parts of ratatouille. Store in the refrigerator for up to 4 days.

 **Reheat** To reheat, microwave for 1 to 2 minutes.

TIP Add a bit of cooked barley or farro to your prep containers for an even more filling meal.

Per Serving (1 container): Calories: 304; Fat: 18g; Protein: 24g; Total Carbs: 14g; Fiber: 5g; Sodium: 102mg; Iron: 1mg

Greek Turkey Burgers

GLUTEN-FREE OPTION, NUT-FREE

PREP 15 minutes · **COOK** 10 minutes · **MAKES** 4 servings

Most people think of Greece when they hear "Mediterranean." These burgers are a favorite for me and my husband. Sun-dried tomatoes add the perfect flavor boost, and they contain vitamin C, lycopene, and lutein, which are powerful antioxidants. I recommend using the tomatoes jarred in olive oil because they help keep the burger moist, but feel free to use dried ones if you prefer.

For the salad

4 cups chopped curly kale

¼ red onion, thinly sliced

1 tablespoon extra-virgin olive oil

Pinch sea salt

For the turkey patties

1 pound ground turkey

1 cup crumbled feta cheese

⅓ cup chopped sun-dried tomatoes

1 teaspoon dried oregano

¼ teaspoon garlic powder

Nonstick olive oil cooking spray

2 (4-inch) whole-wheat pita bread rounds, halved (optional)

1. To make the salad, in a large bowl, combine the kale, red onion, olive oil, and salt. Using your hands, massage the oil into the kale. Set aside.

2. To make the turkey patties, in a large bowl, combine the ground turkey, feta cheese, sun-dried tomatoes, oregano, and garlic powder. Mix well with your hands or a spoon. Form the mixture into 4 even patties.

3. Heat a large cast iron skillet (or your grill) over medium heat. Spray with a touch of cooking spray. Cook the burgers for about 4 minutes on each side.

4. Into each of 4 containers, place even amounts of salad mixture and 1 burger. If using pita, add a half piece of pita to each container. When ready to eat, fill the pita with the salad mixture and a warmed burger.

5. Store the airtight containers in the refrigerator for up to 4 days.

Reheat To reheat the burger, microwave for 1 minute or warm in a cast iron skillet.

Freeze The burgers can be frozen, wrapped individually, for up to 4 months.

Per Serving (1 container): Calories: 338; Fat: 20g; Protein: 30g; Total Carbs: 12g; Fiber: 2g; Sodium: 601mg; Iron: 2mg

Pesto Pasta Salad with Halloumi, page 59

PREP 5

BEAT THE HEAT

When summer arrives, you'll probably want to spend as little time in the kitchen as possible. This week is all about preps that require minimal cooking so that you can enjoy more outside time, which is why I recommend taking a shortcut and picking up a rotisserie chicken to make a salad that is perfect for lunches or summer barbecues. This prep also highlights the vibrant produce of summer with simple preparations of corn, tomatoes, and herbs. Throw any of the meals in a picnic basket with a bottle of rosé and enjoy some newfound time with your partner.

Day	Lunch	Dinner
M	Golden Falafel Bowl	Raw Corn Salad with Seared Mahi Mahi
T	Pesto Pasta Salad with Halloumi	Raw Corn Salad with Seared Mahi Mahi
W	Curry Chicken Salad Wrap	Golden Falafel Bowl
TH	Curry Chicken Salad Wrap	Pesto Pasta Salad with Halloumi
F	Golden Falafel Bowl	Curry Chicken Salad Wrap

SHOPPING LIST

Pantry

- ☐ Chickpeas, low-sodium, 2 (15.5-ounce) cans
- ☐ Flour, all-purpose (or oat flour)
- ☐ Maple syrup
- ☐ Mustard, Dijon
- ☐ Nonstick olive oil cooking spray
- ☐ Oil, avocado
- ☐ Oil, olive, extra-virgin
- ☐ Olives, kalamata, pitted (6 ounces)
- ☐ Pasta, cavatappi, 1 (16-ounce) box
- ☐ Pita bread, whole-wheat, 3 (4-inch) rounds (optional)
- ☐ Tahini (6 ounces)
- ☐ Tortillas, whole-wheat, 6 (8-inch) rounds (optional)
- ☐ Vinegar, red wine
- ☐ Walnuts, raw and unsalted (3 tablespoons)

Herbs and Spices

- ☐ Black pepper, whole
- ☐ Chili powder, ground
- ☐ Cumin, ground
- ☐ Curry powder, yellow
- ☐ Salt
- ☐ Sea salt
- ☐ Turmeric, ground

Produce

- ☐ Arugula (2 cups)
- ☐ Bell peppers, orange or yellow (2)
- ☐ Carrots, medium (5)
- ☐ Celery (1 bunch)
- ☐ Cilantro (3 bunches)
- ☐ Corn (6 ears)
- ☐ Garlic (1 head)
- ☐ Lemons (3)
- ☐ Lettuce, Bibb, small (2 heads)
- ☐ Lettuce, romaine, small (1 head)
- ☐ Limes (4)
- ☐ Onion, red (1)
- ☐ Parsley (1 bunch)
- ☐ Radishes (1 bunch)
- ☐ Tomatoes, beefsteak (2)
- ☐ Tomatoes, cherry (1 pint)
- ☐ Tomatoes, plum (3)
- ☐ Zucchini, medium (2)

Protein

- ☐ Mahi mahi, 4 (4-ounce) fillets
- ☐ Rotisserie chicken, 1 (1½-pound) chicken

Dairy

- ☐ Greek yogurt, plain (8 ounces)
- ☐ Halloumi cheese (4 ounces)

EQUIPMENT

- ☐ Baking dish
- ☐ Chef's knife
- ☐ Cutting board
- ☐ Food processor
- ☐ Measuring cups and spoons
- ☐ Mixing bowls
- ☐ Mixing spoons
- ☐ Sauce pot, large
- ☐ Skillets
- ☐ Spatula
- ☐ Tongs
- ☐ Whisk

PREP CONTAINERS

- ☐ **Golden Falafel Bowl:** 6 containers plus 6 small dressing containers
- ☐ **Raw Corn Salad with Seared Mahi Mahi:** 4 glass containers
- ☐ **Pesto Pasta Salad with Halloumi:** 4 containers
- ☐ **Curry Chicken Salad Wrap:** 6 containers

STEP-BY-STEP PREP

Golden Falafel Bowl, page 54	*Raw Corn Salad with Seared Mahi Mahi,* page 56	*Curry Chicken Salad Wrap,* page 58	*Pesto Pasta Salad with Halloumi,* page 59

▶ **START HERE**

Prepare steps ① through step ②. While the falafel are chilling...

Prepare in full.

Prepare in full.

Finish steps ③ through ⑤.

Prepare in full.

Golden Falafel Bowl

GLUTEN-FREE OPTION, NUT-FREE, VEGAN

PREP 20 minutes · **CHILL** 1 hour · **COOK** 15 minutes · **MAKES** 6 servings

Falafel make great meal preps, since you can freeze these little patties and grab a few whenever you want a quick, flavorful, plant-based protein source. But what makes this bowl so golden is what's in the falafel—the mighty turmeric is an anti-inflammatory super spice, especially when combined with black pepper. It gives the chickpeas a nice kick!

For the bowls

½ cup Dijon Tahini Dressing (page 143)

2 small heads Bibb or other green lettuce, roughly torn

2 orange or yellow bell peppers, roughly chopped

3 plum tomatoes, quartered and diced into chunks

1 cup pitted kalamata olives

3 (4-inch) whole-wheat pita bread rounds, cut into quarters (optional)

For the falafel

2 (15.5-ounce) cans low-sodium chickpeas, drained and rinsed

½ cup lightly packed fresh cilantro

▶

1. Prepare the Dijon Tahini Dressing.

2. To make the falafel, in a food processor, combine the chickpeas, cilantro, parsley, lemon juice, garlic, salt, turmeric, pepper, and cumin. Pulse to combine, scraping down the sides of the bowl as needed until thoroughly combined. The dough will be crumbly at this stage. Add 1 tablespoon of flour at a time and pulse to combine until no longer wet and you can mold the dough into a ball without it sticking to your hands. Transfer to a bowl, cover, and refrigerate for 1 hour.

3. Once chilled, scoop out rounded tablespoon-size amounts and gently flatten into 12 discs. Heat a large skillet over medium heat and pour in the avocado oil. Once the oil is shimmering, add a layer of falafel and cook for 4 to 5 minutes until the underside is browned, then flip. Repeat until all the falafel are cooked.

½ cup lightly packed parsley

Juice of 1 lemon (about
  2 tablespoons)

4 garlic cloves, diced

1 teaspoon salt

1 teaspoon turmeric

½ teaspoon freshly ground
  black pepper

½ teaspoon ground cumin

3 to 4 tablespoons all-
  purpose flour (or oat
  flour for gluten-free)

2 tablespoons avocado oil

④ To make the bowls, into each of 6 containers, place 2 falafel, then even amounts of lettuce, bell pepper, tomato, and olives. Into each of 6 small dressing containers, pour about 2 tablespoons of dressing. Store the pita (if using) separately until ready to serve.

⑤ Store the airtight containers in the refrigerator for up to 5 days.

🔥 **Reheat** If preferred, wrap the falafel in a slightly damp paper towel and microwave for 1 to 2 minutes or heat in a skillet coated with cooking spray.

❄ **Freeze** The falafel can be frozen for up to 2 months. To thaw, refrigerate overnight.

Per Serving (1 container): Calories: 571; Fat: 26g; Protein: 16g; Total Carbs: 72g; Fiber: 13g; Sodium: 1532mg; Iron: 6mg

Raw Corn Salad with Seared Mahi Mahi

DAIRY-FREE, GLUTEN-FREE, NUT-FREE

PREP 20 minutes · MARINATE 30 minutes · COOK 15 minutes · MAKES 4 servings

Did you know you could eat corn raw? I was introduced to this concept at my first nutrition job out of college, and I just love how easy it makes prepping. Plus, raw corn holds its crunch a bit better when stored in the refrigerator for a few days. Corn is considered more of a starchy vegetable, so this salad and fish are not paired with a grain, but if one of you needs more to eat after a long day or workout, you could add a side of brown rice or orzo pasta.

For the fish

4 (4-ounce) mahi mahi fillets

Juice of 2 limes

1 tablespoon extra-virgin
olive oil

1 teaspoon ground cumin

½ teaspoon chili powder

Pinch salt

Nonstick olive oil
cooking spray

For the salad

6 corn ears, husks removed
and cleaned

2 beefsteak tomatoes,
coarsely chopped

2 cups grated carrots

1 medium red onion,
finely chopped

▶

1. To make the fish, rinse the fillets and pat dry. In a large, shallow glass baking dish, mix the lime juice, olive oil, cumin, chili powder, and salt. Add the fish and turn to coat. Let marinate for 30 minutes.

2. To make the salad, gather a large and a small bowl. Place the smaller bowl upside down inside the larger bowl. Stand the corn root-side down on the smaller bowl. Using a sharp kitchen knife, slice down along the cob, cutting away the corn kernels and allowing them to fall into the larger bowl. Continue cutting around the cob until no kernels remain. Repeat with the remaining corn cobs. Remove the small bowl, rinse, and set aside.

3. In the large bowl, combine the tomatoes, carrots, red onion, and radishes.

4. In the small bowl, whisk the cilantro, vinegar, and olive oil. Pour the dressing over the salad and toss to coat the ingredients well. Taste and add salt and pepper as desired. Set aside.

½ cup radishes, halved and thinly sliced

½ cup finely chopped fresh cilantro

¼ cup red wine vinegar

2 tablespoons extra-virgin olive oil

Salt

Freshly ground black pepper

⑤ Heat a large skillet over high heat and lightly coat the bottom with cooking spray. Remove 2 fish fillets from the marinade and place them in the pan side by side. After 30 seconds, lower the heat to medium and let the fish sizzle until the underside turns golden brown, 2 to 3 minutes. Using a spatula, carefully flip the fillets and cook for another 2 to 3 minutes. Remove once browned and set aside. Repeat with the remaining fillets.

⑥ Into each of 4 containers, place 1 fish fillet and even amounts of corn salad. Store the airtight containers in the refrigerator for up to 3 days.

🔥 **Reheat** The corn salad can be eaten cold, but the fish would ideally be reheated in the microwave for 1 to 2 minutes or in a 350°F oven until warmed through.

TIP To minimize food waste, the extra radishes can be quick pickled in some vinegar, salt, and boiling water, and stored in the refrigerator for 2 weeks.

Per Serving (1 container): Calories: 333; Fat: 12g; Protein: 26g; Total Carbs: 34g; Fiber: 6g; Sodium: 204mg; Iron: 3mg

Curry Chicken Salad Wrap

GLUTEN-FREE OPTION, NUT-FREE

PREP 10 minutes · **MAKES** 6 servings

When someone tells me that they feel lazy purchasing premade items from the grocery to have for dinner, I tell them that laziness sometimes leads you to the smartest way of doing things. This chicken salad is surely the work of a genius then as it uses a time-saving superstar: rotisserie chicken. When shopping for your bird, choose one that is unflavored as the added seasonings usually contain quite a bit of sodium. At home, remove the skin to avoid saturated fat, which, in excess, may increase your risk of heart disease.

1 (1½-pound) rotisserie chicken, meat removed and torn into shreds

1½ cups shredded carrots

1 cup plain Greek yogurt

3 celery stalks, halved lengthwise and finely chopped

½ cup fresh cilantro, chopped

2 tablespoons extra-virgin olive oil

Juice of 2 limes

3 teaspoons yellow curry powder

¼ teaspoon turmeric

6 romaine lettuce leaves

6 whole-wheat tortillas (optional)

1. In a large bowl, combine the shredded chicken, carrots, yogurt, celery, cilantro, olive oil, lime juice, curry powder, and turmeric. Using tongs or a fork, mix to combine and coat everything with the yogurt. Taste and adjust the seasonings to your liking.

2. Place equal amounts of chicken salad into lettuce leaf wraps, or lay a leaf of lettuce on a whole-wheat wrap (if using) and then top with chicken salad.

3. Into each of 6 containers, place 1 wrap. Store the airtight containers in the refrigerator for up to 4 days.

Reheat Wraps are best enjoyed cold, but the chicken can be reheated on its own for 1 minute in the microwave if desired.

TIP If you prefer to not buy rotisserie chicken, you can cook the chicken yourself. Simply place the breasts in a large sauce pot of boiling water and cook for 15 to 20 minutes or until the chicken reaches an internal temperature of 165°F. Let cool then shred the chicken with a fork.

Per Serving (1 wrap): Calories: 187; Fat: 7g; Protein: 25g; Total Carbs: 5g; Fiber: 1g; Sodium: 85mg; Iron: 1mg

Pesto Pasta Salad with Halloumi

VEGETARIAN

PREP 10 minutes · **COOK** 15 minutes · **MAKES** 4 servings

I always encourage people with picky eater partners to combine healthy foods with sauces you know they love. If you don't want to cook the vegetables in this salad, simply add raw, thinly sliced zucchini, crunchy sugar snap peas, or green beans.

½ cup Lemon Arugula Pesto (page 149)

3 cups dried cavatappi pasta

2 tablespoons extra-virgin olive oil

2 zucchini, halved lengthwise and cut into ½-inch pieces

4 ounces halloumi cheese, cut into 4 slices

1 cup halved cherry tomatoes

1. Prepare the Lemon Arugula Pesto and set aside.

2. Fill a large sauce pot with water and bring to a boil. Cook the pasta according to the package directions until al dente. Drain the pasta, rinse with cold water, and set aside.

3. While the pasta is cooking, heat the olive oil in a medium skillet over medium heat. Add the zucchini and sauté them until they start to brown and soften. Transfer the zucchini to a large bowl and set aside.

4. As the zucchini are cooking, pat each halloumi slice with a paper towel to remove some moisture. Set aside. In the same heated skillet, lay the halloumi slices in a single layer and cook until golden brown on both sides, 2 to 3 minutes per side. Remove the halloumi and chop into bite-size squares.

5. Into the bowl with the zucchini, add the tomatoes, halloumi bites, and cooked pasta. Top with the pesto and use a spoon to mix everything together.

6. Into each of 4 containers, divide even amounts of pasta salad. Store in the refrigerator for up to 5 days.

🔥 **Reheat** Enjoy this pasta salad cold or reheat in the microwave for 1 to 2 minutes.

TIP If you can't find halloumi, a slightly salty cow's milk cheese from Cyprus, add fresh, raw mozzarella pearls instead.

Per Serving (1 container): Calories: 548; Fat: 33g; Protein: 18g; Total Carbs: 47g; Fiber: 3g; Sodium: 376mg; Iron: 3mg

Zesty Beef Meatballs with Bok Choy and Brown Rice, page 68

PREP 6

COLD COMFORT

When winter rolls around, you'll find any excuse to stay warm indoors. This week's prep emphasizes meals and snacks to keep you both feeling cozy. "Dump and cook" breakfasts pay homage to all things pumpkin spice, whereas lunches and snacks emphasize healing spices to stave off cold season. This week's prep also challenges you with two prep days, but don't worry—I've kept the tasks simple!

	Day	Breakfast	Lunch	Snack
PREP DAY #1	M	Chai Spiced Pear Oatmeal Bake	Sweet and Spicy Sweet Potato Chili	Indian Spice Trail Mix
	T	Chai Spiced Pear Oatmeal Bake	Sweet and Spicy Sweet Potato Chili	Indian Spice Trail Mix
	W	Chai Spiced Pear Oatmeal Bake	Sweet and Spicy Sweet Potato Chili	Indian Spice Trail Mix
PREP DAY #2	TH	Pumpkin Quinoa Power Bowl	Zesty Beef Meatballs with Bok Choy and Brown Rice	Rosemary Popcorn
	F	Pumpkin Quinoa Power Bowl	Zesty Beef Meatballs with Bok Choy and Brown Rice	Rosemary Popcorn

SHOPPING LIST

Pantry

- [ ] Almonds (4 cups)
- [ ] Black beans, low-sodium, 2 (14.5-ounce) cans
- [ ] Chai tea bags (3)
- [ ] Cocoa powder, unsweetened
- [ ] Coconut flakes, unsweetened (¾ cups)
- [ ] Coconut milk, full-fat, 1 (13.5-ounce) can
- [ ] Cornstarch or arrowroot powder
- [ ] Dairy-free milk, unsweetened, 1 (32-ounce) carton
- [ ] Flaxseed, ground
- [ ] Hemp seeds
- [ ] Maple syrup
- [ ] Nonstick olive oil cooking spray
- [ ] Oats, old-fashioned (9 ounces)
- [ ] Oil, olive, extra-virgin
- [ ] Oil, sesame, toasted
- [ ] Peanuts
- [ ] Pear halves, no-sugar-added, 1 (14.5-ounce) can
- [ ] Pecans
- [ ] Popcorn kernels
- [ ] Pumpkin purée, 1 (15-ounce) can
- [ ] Quinoa
- [ ] Raisins, golden
- [ ] Rice, brown
- [ ] Soy sauce, low-sodium
- [ ] Sugar, brown
- [ ] Tomatoes, fire-roasted, 2 (14.5-ounce) cans
- [ ] Tomato paste, 1 (6-ounce) can or squeezable pouch
- [ ] Tomato sauce, 2 (14.5-ounce) cans
- [ ] Vegetable broth, low-sodium (4 ounces)

Herbs and Spices

- [ ] Allspice, ground
- [ ] Cardamom, ground
- [ ] Chili powder
- [ ] Cinnamon, ground
- [ ] Cumin, ground
- [ ] Curry powder, yellow
- [ ] Nutmeg, ground
- [ ] Red pepper flakes
- [ ] Rosemary, dried
- [ ] Salt

Produce

- [ ] Bok choy, baby (3 bunches)
- [ ] Cilantro (1 bunch)
- [ ] Garlic (1 head)
- [ ] Jalapeño pepper (1) (optional)
- [ ] Onion, yellow (1)
- [ ] Orange (1)
- [ ] Sweet potatoes, small (2)

Protein

- [ ] Beef, ground (1 pound)
- [ ] Egg, large (1)

Dairy

- [ ] Sour cream (optional)

EQUIPMENT

- [ ] Aluminum foil
- [ ] Baking pan (9-inch square)
- [ ] Baking sheets
- [ ] Chef's knife
- [ ] Cutting board
- [ ] Dutch oven
- [ ] Measuring cups and spoons
- [ ] Mixing bowls
- [ ] Mixing spoons
- [ ] Sauce pots
- [ ] Skillet
- [ ] Tongs
- [ ] Whisk
- [ ] Zester

PREP CONTAINERS

- [ ] **Chai Spiced Pear Oatmeal Bake:** 6 glass containers
- [ ] **Indian Spice Trail Mix:** 6 containers or resealable sandwich bags
- [ ] **Sweet and Spicy Sweet Potato Chili:** 6 glass containers
- [ ] **Zesty Beef Meatballs with Bok Choy and Brown Rice:** 4 glass containers
- [ ] **Rosemary Popcorn:** 4 resealable sandwich bags
- [ ] **Pumpkin Quinoa Power Bowl:** 4 glass containers

STEP-BY-STEP PREP DAY #1

Chai Spiced Pear Oatmeal Bake, *page 65*

Indian Spice Trail Mix, *page 66*

Sweet and Spicy Sweet Potato Chili, *page 67*

▶ START HERE

Prepare steps ① through ④. While the oatmeal is baking...

Prepare in full.

Finish step ⑤.

Prepare in full.

STEP-BY-STEP PREP DAY #2

Zesty Beef Meatballs with Bok Choy and Brown Rice, *page 68*

Rosemary Popcorn, *page 70*

Pumpkin Quinoa Power Bowl, *page 71*

▶ START HERE

Prepare steps ① through ⑤. While the meatballs, bok choy, and rice are cooking...

Prepare in full.

Finish steps ⑥ through ⑧.

Prepare in full.

Chai Spiced Pear Oatmeal Bake

GLUTEN-FREE, NUT-FREE, VEGAN

PREP 10 minutes • **COOK** 25 minutes • **MAKES** 6 servings

Oatmeal and cold weather go together like watermelon and summer. Single flavored packets of oatmeal, however, can be quite high in added sugar and sodium. This meal prep version is healthier and tastier as well as simple to make. If you're gluten free, look for a gluten-free label on your oats.

Nonstick olive oil cooking spray

3 cups unsweetened dairy-free milk (almond, soy, or oat)

3 chai tea bags

1 (14.5-ounce) can no-sugar-added pear halves, drained

3 cups old-fashioned oats

2 tablespoons ground flaxseed

1 tablespoon ground cinnamon

2 teaspoons ground cardamom

½ teaspoon salt

1 tablespoon brown sugar

① Preheat the oven to 350°F. Spray the bottom and sides of a 9-inch square baking dish with cooking spray.

② In a medium pot, bring the dairy-free milk to a simmer. Once simmering, turn off the heat and add the tea bags. Steep for 5 minutes then remove the tea bags.

③ While the tea steeps, in a large bowl, place the pears and use the back of a fork to mash them into a purée. To the bowl, add the oats, flaxseed, cinnamon, cardamom, and salt. Pour the chai-infused milk into the bowl and use a spoon to mix together.

④ Transfer the mixture to the baking dish and sprinkle the brown sugar across the surface. Bake for 25 minutes, until everything appears to have set.

⑤ Remove from the oven, let cool, and divide the oatmeal bake into 6 equal squares. Into each of 6 containers, place 1 baked square. Store the covered containers in the refrigerator for up to 4 days.

Reheat Reheat in the microwave for about 2 minutes or in the oven at 350°F for about 10 minutes.

Freeze Freeze for up to 2 months. To thaw, refrigerate overnight.

Per Serving (1 oatmeal square): Calories: 226; Fat: 5g; Protein: 7g; Total Carbs: 39g; Fiber: 7g; Sodium: 292mg; Iron: 3mg

Indian Spice Trail Mix

GLUTEN-FREE, VEGAN

PREP 5 minutes · **MAKES** 6 servings

Balanced snacks are something I always discuss with my patients—and partner. You simply feel satisfied for a longer period of time when you eat snacks that have a combination of nutrients. So, this sweet and salty trail mix combines protein, healthy fats, carbohydrates, and cold-fighting spices. It also quickly feeds two hungry people in search of something to munch on.

1½ cups golden raisins

¾ cup peanuts

¾ cup almonds

6 tablespoons unsweetened coconut flakes

3 teaspoons yellow curry powder

1½ teaspoons ground cinnamon

1. In a large bowl, combine the raisins, peanuts, almonds, coconut flakes, curry powder, and cinnamon. Shake or stir everything together to mix well.

2. Into each of 6 containers, divide the mixture evenly.

3. Store in airtight containers in the pantry for up to 3 months.

TIP The combination of nuts, seeds, and fun things are endless for trail mix. This blend would also work well with pistachios instead of peanuts and banana chips instead of raisins.

Per Serving (1 container): Calories: 321; Fat: 23g; Protein: 9g; Total Carbs: 24g; Fiber: 6g; Sodium: 11mg; Iron: 2mg

Sweet and Spicy Sweet Potato Chili

GLUTEN-FREE, NUT-FREE, VEGAN

PREP 10 minutes · **COOK** 40 minutes · **MAKES** 6 servings

If there's one thing I know for sure, it's that a pot of chili is the ultimate winter meal prep for two. This batch will keep you warm and nourished for days! My version skips the meat and uses black beans and sweet potatoes for bulk. I add spicy chili powder but also tomato paste and some cocoa powder for sweetness, just like we did back home in Cincinnati.

2 tablespoons extra-virgin olive oil

4 cups sweet potato (about 2 small potatoes), cut into 1-inch cubes

1 yellow onion, chopped

2 garlic cloves, minced

2 tablespoons tomato paste

2 (14.5-ounce) cans low-sodium black beans, drained and rinsed

2 (14.5-ounce) cans fire-roasted tomatoes, drained

2 (14.5-ounce) cans tomato sauce

1 tablespoon ground cumin

2 teaspoons chili powder

1 teaspoon unsweetened cocoa powder

Cilantro, for garnish (optional)

Sliced or pickled jalapeño peppers, for garnish (optional)

Sour cream, for garnish (optional)

1. In a large Dutch oven or pot, heat the olive oil over medium heat. When the oil is shimmering, sauté the sweet potatoes and onion for 5 minutes, then add the garlic. Sauté for 3 more minutes.

2. Add the tomato paste and stir gently for 1 minute until the paste darkens in color. Next add the black beans, roasted tomatoes, tomato sauce, cumin, chili powder, and cocoa powder. Stir and cover.

3. Return the pot to a simmer and cook, covered. After 25 minutes, stir and add more water if you prefer a thinner chili. Taste and adjust the spice and sweetness as well. Add a pinch of salt if desired. Cover and cook for 5 more minutes. Remove from heat and allow to cool.

4. Into each of 6 containers, divide equal amounts of chili (about 1½-cup servings). If desired, top with, or store separately, cilantro, jalapeños, or sour cream.

5. Store the airtight containers in the refrigerator for up to 5 days.

Reheat Reheat in the microwave for 2 minutes or on the stovetop.

Freeze Freeze for up to 3 months. To thaw, refrigerate overnight.

Per Serving (1 container): Calories: 307; Fat: 6g; Protein: 15g; Total Carbs: 53g; Fiber: 16g; Sodium: 568mg; Iron: 6mg

Zesty Beef Meatballs with Bok Choy and Brown Rice

DAIRY-FREE, GLUTEN-FREE OPTION, NUT-FREE

PREP 10 minutes · **COOK** 50 minutes · **MAKES** 4 servings

Eating vitamin C–rich foods like citrus and bok choy can give you an immunity boost in the winter and help ward off a cold. These meatballs are simple enough to mix in one bowl and bake, but you could pick up some premade frozen beef or chicken meatballs to save even more time when cooking for two. Precooked frozen brown rice would also make this meal even easier.

For the meatballs

1 pound ground beef

½ cup finely chopped fresh cilantro

1 large egg

4 garlic cloves, minced

2 tablespoons low-sodium soy sauce (or tamari for gluten-free)

3 bunches baby bok choy, root ends cut off, sliced lengthwise

2 tablespoons extra-virgin olive oil, divided

Pinch salt

1 cup brown rice

2½ cups water

For the sauce

2 tablespoons cornstarch or arrowroot powder

2 tablespoons cold water

▶

1. Preheat the oven to 375°F. Line two baking sheets with aluminum foil.

2. To make the meatballs, in a medium bowl, combine the ground beef, cilantro, egg, garlic, and soy sauce. Using your hands, mix everything together, then roll the mixture into 1-inch balls until you have about 12 meatballs. Place the finished meatballs on one prepared baking sheet.

3. On the other baking sheet, lay the bok choy evenly and drizzle 1 tablespoon of olive oil on top. Season with a pinch of salt.

4. Bake the meatballs for 15 to 20 minutes until browned and cooked through. Roast the bok choy for 15 minutes, then turn over and roast for another 15 minutes until crispy and browned. Remove from the oven and set aside.

5. While the meatballs and bok choy are cooking, prepare the brown rice. Heat a medium sauce pot over medium heat and add the remaining 1 tablespoon of olive oil and the rice. Sauté for 1 minute, then pour in the water and bring to a boil. Cover and simmer for about 40 minutes. Remove from the heat, keeping the pan covered, and let sit 10 minutes. Fluff the rice with a fork and set aside.

½ cup low-sodium
   vegetable broth

¼ cup low-sodium soy sauce
   (or tamari for gluten-free)

Juice of 1 orange
   (about ⅓ cup juice)

2 tablespoons toasted
   sesame oil

1 tablespoon grated
   orange zest

½ teaspoon red pepper flakes

⑥ To make the sauce, in a small bowl, whisk the cornstarch and cold water. Mix well to form a smooth paste. In another small bowl, mix the vegetable broth, soy sauce, orange juice, sesame oil, orange zest, and red pepper flakes. Pour this into a medium skillet and bring to a low simmer. Once simmering, add the cornstarch paste and whisk well until the sauce thickens.

⑦ Add the cooked meatballs to the sauce and use tongs to turn and coat them in the sauce.

⑧ Into each of 4 containers, place 1 cup of brown rice, even amounts of roasted bok choy, and 3 meatballs with sauce. Store in the refrigerator for up to 4 days.

 **Reheat** To reheat, microwave for 1 to 2 minutes.

❄ **Freeze** Freeze for up to 3 months. To thaw, refrigerate overnight.

Per Serving (1 container): Calories: 515; Fat: 24g; Protein: 31g; Total Carbs: 46g; Fiber: 3g; Sodium: 1548mg; Iron: 4mg

Rosemary Popcorn

GLUTEN-FREE, NUT-FREE, VEGAN

PREP 1 minute · **COOK** 10 minutes · **MAKES** 4 servings

Did you know that popcorn is a whole grain? Air-popped popcorn is a top nutritious snack in our house. One cup has only 30 calories but contains 1 whole gram of fiber, and a serving for one person is roughly 3 cups, making this a great volume snack. Popping your own is a great way to be in control of the fat and sodium content as well.

½ teaspoon dried rosemary

¼ teaspoon salt

2 tablespoons, extra-virgin olive oil, plus 2 teaspoons

½ cup popcorn kernels

1. In a small bowl, whisk together the rosemary, salt, and 2 tablespoons of olive oil. Set aside.

2. In a large Dutch oven or pot, heat the remaining 2 teaspoons of olive oil over medium heat. When the oil is shimmering, drop a corn kernel into the pot and watch for it to sizzle. If it does, the oil is hot enough and you may add the remaining kernels.

3. Immediately cover the pot with a tight-fitting lid and begin to shake the pot back and forth over the heat source. Continue quickly moving the pot back and forth until all of the kernels have popped.

4. Drizzle the rosemary and olive oil dressing over the warm kernels, tossing to coat well.

5. Into each of 4 (1-quart) resealable bags, place 3 cups of popcorn and seal tightly. Store in an airtight bag for up to 2 days.

TIP Pop a large batch and let each person choose their preferred seasonings. Oregano, chili powder, curry, and cinnamon all would work well.

Per Serving (3 cups popcorn): Calories: 97; Fat: 10g; Protein: 0g; Total Carbs: 2g; Fiber: 3g; Sodium: 171mg; Iron: 0mg

Pumpkin Quinoa Power Bowl

GLUTEN-FREE, VEGAN

PREP 5 minutes · **COOK** 20 minutes · **MAKES** 4 servings

For those who don't love oatmeal (or get sick of it sometimes), this power bowl introduces a new grain for breakfast. This sweet version of a quinoa porridge uses canned pumpkin as a convenient way to add in a vitamin C–rich vegetable during the winter cold season.

1 cup unsweetened dairy-free milk (almond, soy, or oat)

½ cup water

1 cup dried quinoa, rinsed

1⅓ cups pumpkin purée

1 cup coconut milk, divided

1 tablespoon maple syrup

1 teaspoon ground cinnamon

½ teaspoon ground nutmeg

½ teaspoon ground allspice

1 cup chopped pecans

¼ cup hemp seeds

Maple syrup, for serving (optional)

1. In a large pot, bring the dairy-free milk and water to a boil. Add the quinoa, reduce the heat to low, and cover the pot.

2. After 7 to 8 minutes, add the pumpkin purée and ½ cup of coconut milk. Stir to combine. Replace the lid to continue cooking for another 7 to 8 minutes until the quinoa is fluffy.

3. Turn off the heat and add the remaining ½ cup of coconut milk, maple syrup, cinnamon, nutmeg, and allspice. Stir to combine.

4. Into each of 4 containers, spoon equal amounts of porridge and top each with ¼ cup of pecans, 1 tablespoon of hemp seeds, and an extra drizzle of maple syrup, if desired.

5. Store the airtight containers in the refrigerator for up to 4 days.

Reheat To reheat, microwave for 1 to 2 minutes.

Freeze Freeze for up to 2 months. To thaw, refrigerate overnight.

TIP You can use the entire can of pumpkin purée in this recipe if you'd like; otherwise, the small amount that's left over can easily be stirred into soups or pasta bakes or used for Pumpkin Yogurt Dip (page 157).

Per Serving (1 container): Calories: 590; Fat: 41g; Protein: 15g; Total Carbs: 48g; Fiber: 11g; Sodium: 109mg; Iron: 6mg

Stone Fruit and Grilled Chicken (Chickpea) Salad Jars, page 83

PREP 7

FLEXITARIAN

Can meal prepping work when one of you eats meat and the other doesn't? Absolutely. And it's actually easier than you may think. Most of this week's meals start with a grain and some vegetables and end with the addition of a protein source, allowing each person to add their preference without changing up the rest of the dish very much. All breakfasts are vegetarian to keep it simple!

	Day	Breakfast	Lunch	Dinner
PREP DAY #1	M	Berries and Yogurt Muesli Cups	Stone Fruit and Grilled Chicken (Chickpea) Salad Jars	Baked Salmon (Tempeh) with Cauliflower Freekeh Pilaf
	T	Berries and Yogurt Muesli Cups	Stone Fruit and Grilled Chicken (Chickpea) Salad Jars	Cajun Quinoa Jambalaya with Sausage (Red Beans)
	W	Berries and Yogurt Muesli Cups	Baked Salmon (Tempeh) with Cauliflower Freekeh Pilaf	Cajun Quinoa Jambalaya with Sausage (Red Beans)
PREP DAY #2	TH	Southwestern Egg Scramble	Ramen Noodle Cups with Chicken (Tofu and Edamame)	DIY Steak (Black Bean) Fajita Bowls
	F	Southwestern Egg Scramble	Ramen Noodle Cups with Chicken (Tofu and Edamame)	DIY Steak (Black Bean) Fajita Bowls

SHOPPING LIST

Pantry

- ☐ Asian noodles (ramen, soba, somen, or udon) (12 ounces)
- ☐ Black beans, low-sodium, 2 (15.5-ounce) cans
- ☐ Bouillon paste, vegetable, 1 (3-ounce) tube
- ☐ Brown rice, instant cook, 1 (14-ounce) box
- ☐ Capers (3 tablespoons)
- ☐ Chickpeas, low-sodium, 1 (14.5-ounce) can
- ☐ Freekeh (1 cup)
- ☐ Honey
- ☐ Miso paste, white
- ☐ Muesli, 1 (14-ounce) package
- ☐ Nonstick olive oil cooking spray
- ☐ Oil, avocado
- ☐ Oil, olive, extra-virgin
- ☐ Oil, sesame, toasted
- ☐ Quinoa (5 cups)
- ☐ Red beans, low-sodium, 1 (14.5-ounce) can
- ☐ Sesame seeds (optional)
- ☐ Soy sauce, low-sodium
- ☐ Tomatoes, crushed, 2 (14-ounce) cans
- ☐ Vegetable broth, low-sodium (40 ounces)
- ☐ Vinegar, balsamic
- ☐ Vinegar, rice wine

Herbs and Spices

- ☐ Black pepper, whole
- ☐ Cayenne pepper
- ☐ Chili powder
- ☐ Cumin, ground
- ☐ Oregano, dried
- ☐ Paprika, sweet
- ☐ Salt

Produce

- ☐ Arugula, 2 (6-ounce) bags
- ☐ Avocado, medium (1)
- ☐ Bell peppers, green (3)
- ☐ Bell peppers, red (2)
- ☐ Bell pepper, yellow (1)
- ☐ Carrots, shredded, 1 (10-ounce) bag
- ☐ Cauliflower rice, 1 (12-ounce) bag
- ☐ Celery (1 bunch)
- ☐ Chile pepper, red (1)
- ☐ Cilantro (1 bunch)
- ☐ Garlic (1 head)
- ☐ Lemon (1)
- ☐ Lime (1)
- ☐ Mushrooms, cremini (7 ounces)
- ☐ Mushrooms, portobello, baby (4)
- ☐ Nectarines (2)
- ☐ Onion, red (1)
- ☐ Onion, white (1)
- ☐ Onions, yellow (2)
- ☐ Parsley (1 bunch)

- ☐ Peaches (2)
- ☐ Pico de gallo, 1 (12-ounce) container
- ☐ Poblano pepper (1)
- ☐ Potatoes, small red (12 ounces)
- ☐ Scallions (1 bunch)
- ☐ Shallots (2)
- ☐ Zucchini, medium (1)

Frozen

- ☐ Corn, 1 (10-ounce) bag
- ☐ Edamame, 1 (10-ounce) bag
- ☐ Mixed berries (30 ounces)

Protein

- ☐ Andouille sausage, precooked (2 links)
- ☐ Beef, flank steak, 1 (8-ounce)
- ☐ Chicken breast, thinly sliced, boneless, skinless (1½ pounds)
- ☐ Eggs, large (4)
- ☐ Salmon, 2 (4-ounce) fillets
- ☐ Tempeh, 1 (8-ounce) package
- ☐ Tofu, firm, 1 (12-ounce) package

Dairy

- ☐ Feta cheese (3 ounces)
- ☐ Greek yogurt, 1 (32-ounce) and 1 (16-ounce) container
- ☐ Pepper Jack cheese (4 ounces)

EQUIPMENT

- ☐ Baking dish
- ☐ Baking sheet
- ☐ Chef's knife
- ☐ Cutting board
- ☐ Dutch oven
- ☐ Grater/shredder
- ☐ Measuring cups and spoons
- ☐ Microwave-safe bowl
- ☐ Mixing bowls
- ☐ Mixing spoon
- ☐ Sauce pots
- ☐ Skillet
- ☐ Spatula
- ☐ Whisk

PREP CONTAINERS

- ☐ **Baked Salmon (Tempeh) with Cauliflower Freekeh Pilaf:** 4 glass containers
- ☐ **Berries and Yogurt Muesli Cups:** 6 containers
- ☐ **Cajun Quinoa Jambalaya with Sausage (Red Beans):** 4 glass containers
- ☐ **Stone Fruit and Grilled Chicken (Chickpea) Salad Jars:** 4 containers
- ☐ **Southwestern Egg Scramble:** 4 glass containers
- ☐ **Ramen Noodle Cups with Chicken (Tofu and Edamame):** 4 glass containers
- ☐ **DIY Steak (Black Bean) Fajita Bowls:** 4 glass containers

STEP-BY-STEP PREP DAY #1

Baked Salmon (Tempeh) with Cauliflower Freekeh Pilaf, page 78	*Berries and Yogurt Muesli Cups,* page 80	*Cajun Quinoa Jambalaya with Sausage (Red Beans),* page 81	*Stone Fruit and Grilled Chicken (Chickpea) Salad Jars,* page 83

► START HERE

Prepare steps ① through ⑤. While the salmon and tempeh are in the oven . . .

Prepare in full.

Finish step ⑥.

Prepare in full.

Prepare in full.

STEP-BY-STEP PREP DAY #2

| **Southwestern Egg Scramble,** page 84 | **Ramen Noodle Cups with Chicken (Tofu and Edamame),** page 85 | **DIY Steak (Black Bean) Fajita Bowls,** page 87 |

▶ START HERE

Prepare steps ① through ②. While the potatoes are roasting . . .

Prepare steps ① through ③. When the potatoes are done, increase the oven temperature to 375°F . . .

Prepare steps ② through ④.

Finish steps ④ through ⑤.

Finish step ⑤.

Finish steps ③ through ④.

Baked Salmon *(Tempeh)* with Cauliflower Freekeh Pilaf

DAIRY-FREE, NUT-FREE *(NUT-FREE, VEGAN)*

PREP 5 min · **MARINATE** 30 min · **COOK** 30 min · **MAKES** 4 servings (2 per variety)

If you're getting tired of brown rice and quinoa in your meal preps, maybe it's time to get *freekeh*. This twist on a pilaf uses freekeh, which is a young green wheat that gets roasted, resulting in a slightly chewy, toasty grain. Compared to quinoa, freekeh has more protein and twice the amount of fiber, perfect for partners who are looking to get healthy together. There's also some cauliflower rice mixed in here, since it adds a lot of volume to a meal without adding a ton of calories or fat. Feel free to double the amount for an extra-filling meal.

For the proteins

3 tablespoons soy sauce (or tamari for gluten-free)

2 tablespoons extra-virgin olive oil

Juice of ½ lemon

¼ teaspoon freshly ground black pepper

2 (4-ounce) salmon fillets

6 ounces tempeh, cut into 8 (¼-inch) slices

For the pilaf

1 tablespoon extra-virgin olive oil

2 shallots, diced

1 cup freekeh

1 garlic clove, minced

⅛ teaspoon freshly ground black pepper

¼ teaspoon dried oregano

▶

① Preheat the oven to 375°F.

② In a small bowl, whisk together the soy sauce, olive oil, lemon juice, and pepper. Lay the salmon fillets and tempeh slices in a baking dish and pour the sauce over the proteins to coat. Marinate for 30 minutes at room temperature.

③ To make the pilaf, heat a large sauce pot over medium heat and pour in the olive oil. When the oil is shimmering, add the shallots and sauté for 3 minutes. When the shallots have softened, add the freekeh, garlic, pepper, and oregano and sauté for 1 minute to toast the grain. Pour in the vegetable broth, cover, and simmer for 15 to 20 minutes until the liquid is absorbed and the grains are soft.

④ While the freekeh is simmering, in a loosely covered bowl, steam the cauliflower rice in the microwave for 4 minutes. When the freekeh has finished cooking, add the cauliflower rice to the pot, along with the parsley, capers, and lemon juice. Stir to combine, season with salt, and set aside.

1 cup low-sodium
vegetable broth

1 (12-ounce) bag riced
cauliflower

½ cup chopped parsley

3 tablespoons capers

Juice of ½ lemon

Salt

⑤ Strain the marinade from the baking dish and discard it. Place the proteins in the oven to bake for 20 to 25 minutes, flipping the tempeh over halfway through. The salmon and tempeh should both appear browned when complete.

⑥ Into each of 4 containers, place a piece of salmon or 4 slices of tempeh, and about 1¼ cups of pilaf. Store the airtight containers in the refrigerator up for to 4 days.

🔥 **Reheat** Reheat in the microwave for 2 minutes.

❄️ **Freeze** You can freeze the pilaf for up to 2 months. To thaw, refrigerate overnight. Reheat in the microwave for 2 minutes.

Per Serving (1 container with salmon): Calories: 502; Fat: 27g; Protein: 35g; Total Carbs: 35g; Fiber: 7g; Sodium: 1043mg; Iron: 3mg

Per Serving (1 container with tempeh): Calories: 430; Fat: 19g; Protein: 28g; Total Carbs: 43g; Fiber: 7g; Sodium: 947mg; Iron: 3mg

Berries and Yogurt Muesli Cups

VEGETARIAN

PREP 10 minutes · **MAKES** 6 servings

Most people are huge fans of granola but haven't ever tried muesli. Muesli is granola's healthier Swiss cousin—a mixture of wheat, oats, nuts, and dried fruit that's often lower in added sugars. It's traditionally eaten soaked in milk with grated apple. Here, the muesli is nestled in some protein-rich Greek yogurt and topped with mixed berries. If one of you is lactose intolerant or vegan, choose your favorite dairy-free or plant-based yogurt instead.

Per container (x6)

¾ cup muesli

1 cup plain Greek yogurt

1 cup mixed berries (frozen)

1. Into each of 6 containers, place the muesli on the bottom, then the yogurt, and top with the berries.

2. Store the airtight containers in the refrigerator for up to 5 days.

❄ **Freeze** Freeze for up to 1 month. To thaw, refrigerate overnight.

TIP If you'd prefer to make homemade muesli, it's easy—just combine four parts rolled grain, one part nuts/seeds, one part dried fruit, and whatever spices your heart desires. A favorite combo of mine is old-fashioned oats, walnuts, dried cherries, cinnamon, and unsweetened coconut flakes.

Per Serving (1 container): Calories: 299; Fat: 3g; Protein: 21g; Total Carbs: 53g; Fiber: 7g; Sodium: 166mg; Iron: 2mg

Cajun Quinoa Jambalaya with Sausage *(Red Beans)*

DAIRY-FREE, GLUTEN-FREE, NUT-FREE *(GLUTEN-FREE, NUT-FREE, VEGAN)*

PREP 5 minutes · **COOK** 20 minutes · **MAKES** 4 servings (2 of each variety)

Jambalaya is a quintessential New Orleans dish that many would say *must* contain sausage and seafood, but I'm challenging that idea with this one-pot quinoa jambalaya, adaptable for a vegetarian or vegan. Traditional andouille sausage is used in one variation—find these sausages precooked to save an extra cooking step—and hearty red beans are tossed in for the other. Both versions contain ample flavor and spice, which can even be adjusted for you and your partner's taste buds.

2 tablespoons extra-virgin olive oil

2 green bell peppers, chopped

1 red bell pepper, chopped

1 medium white onion, chopped (about 1 cup)

2 celery stalks, sliced lengthwise and chopped

4 garlic cloves, minced

1 zucchini, chopped into ¼-inch pieces

4 cups low-sodium vegetable broth

2 (14-ounce) cans crushed tomatoes

1 cup dried quinoa, rinsed

1 teaspoon sweet paprika

½ teaspoon cayenne pepper

½ teaspoon salt

¼ teaspoon freshly ground black pepper

▶

① In a Dutch oven or large pot, heat the olive oil over medium heat. When the oil is shimmering, add the bell peppers, onion, celery, and garlic. Sauté for 5 minutes. Add in the zucchini. Cook for another 3 to 5 minutes until the zucchini starts to soften.

② Next add in the vegetable broth, tomatoes and their juices, quinoa, paprika, cayenne, salt, and pepper. Stir to combine and then cover and let cook for 10 to 12 minutes.

③ While the base is cooking, drain and rinse the red beans and set aside. Prepare the sausages by gently sautéing them in a small skillet until heated through, 7 to 8 minutes.

④ After 10 minutes, check the quinoa for doneness—it should be springy and have absorbed a good amount of the broth. Adjust the seasonings as desired.

▶

1 (14.5-ounce) can low-sodium red beans, drained and rinsed

2 precooked andouille sausages, cut into ½-inch rounds

⑤ Into each of 4 containers, place about 1½ cups of quinoa jambalaya. In 2 of the containers, place equal amounts of cooked sausage rounds, and into the other 2 containers, place about 1 cup of red beans.

⑥ Store the airtight containers in the refrigerator for up to 4 days.

🔥 **Reheat** Reheat in the microwave for 1 to 2 minutes or on the stovetop until heated through, 5 to 7 minutes.

❄️ **Freeze** Freeze for up to 3 months. To thaw, refrigerate overnight.

TIP Rinsing quinoa removes the bitter outer layer. Some varieties sold are prerinsed.

Per Serving (1 container with sausage)**:** Calories: 593; Fat: 28g; Protein: 28g; Total Carbs: 59g; Fiber: 12g; Sodium: 1560mg; Iron: 7g

Per Serving (1 container with red beans)**:** Calories: 531; Fat: 10g; Protein: 25g; Total Carbs: 86g; Fiber: 19g; Sodium: 1018mg; Iron: 7g

Stone Fruit and Grilled Chicken
(Chickpea) *Salad Jars*

GLUTEN-FREE, NUT-FREE *(GLUTEN-FREE, NUT-FREE, VEGETARIAN)*

PREP 10 minutes • **COOK** 10 minutes • **MAKES** 4 servings (2 of each variety)

Stone fruit—any fruit with a large, hard seed in the middle—reach peak ripeness and flavor during the summer months. These salads are conveniently assembled into quart-size mason jars with either grilled chicken or fresh chickpeas, depending on protein preference. But the feta cheese and balsamic dressing are nonnegotiable!

For the chicken

Nonstick olive oil
  cooking spray

For the dressing

¼ cup extra-virgin olive oil

2 tablespoons
  balsamic vinegar

1 teaspoon honey

Pinch salt

Freshly ground black pepper

Per container (x4)

½ cup low-sodium canned
  chickpeas, drained and
  rinsed, or 4 ounces grilled
  chicken breast, cut into
  bite-size cubes

3 tablespoons crumbled
  feta cheese

¼ cup red onion, halved and
  thinly sliced

¾ cup chopped peaches and
  nectarines (2 peaches and
  2 nectarines total)

2 cups arugula

1. Heat a medium skillet over medium heat. Coat the pan with cooking spray and add the chicken breasts. Cook for 3 to 4 minutes per side, until they reach an internal temperature of 165°F. Let the chicken cool, then cut it into bite-size cubes.

2. To make the dressing, in a small bowl, whisk the olive oil, balsamic vinegar, and honey and season with salt and pepper.

3. Into each of 4 containers, first pour in 2 tablespoons of dressing. Then add the chickpeas or grilled chicken, followed by the feta, red onion, fruit, and finally the arugula.

4. When ready to eat, dump the contents into a bowl and mix well. Store in airtight containers in the refrigerator for up to 4 days.

TIP Chickpeas are not a complete source of protein, meaning some of the essential amino acids are not present. Be sure to consume other grains, like quinoa, corn, or brown rice, at other meals in the day to complement the missing protein in these legumes.

Per Serving (1 container with chicken): Calories: 343; Fat: 22g; Protein: 30g; Total Carbs: 7g; Fiber: 1g; Sodium: 207mg; Iron: 1mg

Per Serving (1 container with chickpeas): Calories: 214; Fat: 15g; Protein: 5g; Total Carbs: 18g; Fiber: 1g; Sodium: 231mg; Iron: 3mg

Southwestern Egg Scramble

GLUTEN-FREE, NUT-FREE, VEGETARIAN

PREP 15 minutes • **COOK** 20 minutes • **MAKES** 4 servings

If you're thinking of skipping over this recipe because you'll have to reheat eggs and you worry they'll become rubbery, keep reading! This egg scramble is kept moist during storage and reheating thanks to the perfect initial cooking time of the eggs, the meaty mushrooms, and the saucy pico de gallo.

12 ounces small red potatoes, quartered

3 tablespoons extra-virgin olive oil, divided

Pinch salt

½ yellow onion, chopped

2 cups sliced cremini mushrooms

1 poblano pepper, chopped

2 large eggs, beaten

2 large egg whites, beaten

1 (15.5-ounce) can low-sodium black beans, drained and rinsed

1 cup pico de gallo

1 cup shredded pepper Jack cheese

① Preheat the oven to 350°F.

② In a medium baking dish, place the potatoes and add 2 tablespoons of olive oil and a pinch of salt. Using your hands or a mixing spoon, stir to coat the potatoes, then spread them in a flat layer. Roast the potatoes until you can easily pierce them with a fork, 15 to 20 minutes. Remove from the oven and set aside.

③ Heat the remaining 1 tablespoon of olive oil in a large skillet over medium heat. Add the onion and cook until it starts to soften, about 3 minutes. Add the mushrooms and poblano pepper and continue cooking, stirring occasionally, for about 5 minutes. Add the eggs and egg whites and cook, stirring slowly, for about 3 minutes. The eggs should retain some of their liquid and not be cooked to fully dry.

④ Into each of 4 containers, place a quarter of the potatoes and egg mixture, about ¼ cup of black beans, and ¼ cup of pico de gallo. Top each with ¼ cup of shredded pepper Jack cheese. Store in the refrigerator for up to 3 days.

Reheat Reheat in the microwave for 30-second intervals until warmed through, about 1 minute.

TIP Adapt this scramble to use up whatever vegetable odds and ends you have in your refrigerator, to avoid food waste.

Per Serving (1 container): Calories: 454; Fat: 26g; Protein: 19g; Total Carbs: 40g; Fiber: 8g; Sodium: 613mg; Iron: 3mg

Ramen Noodle Cups with Chicken
(Tofu and Edamame)

DAIRY-FREE, NUT-FREE *(NUT-FREE, VEGAN)*

PREP 5 minutes · **COOK** 20 minutes · **MAKES** 4 servings (2 of each variety)

I think everyone can remember at least one night in college when ramen noodles came to the rescue. Well, I'm bringing them back, but say hello to the healthier and tastier adult version! These cups contain less sodium and preservatives and more vegetables than the store-bought version as well as a protein source for a more balanced meal. For the noodles, you may choose whatever variety you please, such as ramen, soba, somen, or udon.

For the ramen base

1 tablespoon white miso paste

1 tablespoon rice wine vinegar

1 tablespoon low-sodium soy sauce

2 tablespoons toasted sesame oil

2 tablespoons diced fresh red chile pepper

8 ounces boneless, skinless chicken breasts, thinly sliced

12 ounces Asian noodles

6 ounces firm tofu, cut into ½-inch cubes

1 cup shelled edamame (fresh or frozen)

Per container (x4)

1 teaspoon vegetable bouillon paste

⅓ cup shredded carrots

▶

1. In a medium bowl, prepare the ramen base by whisking together the miso paste, rice wine vinegar, soy sauce, sesame oil, and red chile. Set aside.

2. Bring a medium pot of water to a boil and cook the chicken for 15 to 20 minutes, until the internal temperature reaches 165°F. Let cool and slice thinly or shred using a fork.

3. While the chicken is cooking, bring a large pot of water to a boil and cook the noodles according to the package instructions. Drain and set aside.

4. Into each of 4 containers, put 3 tablespoons of ramen liquid base into the bottom. Next add in the bouillon, carrots, corn, and mushroom, followed by the cooked noodles. Top with the cilantro, scallions, and sesame seeds (if using). Into 2 of the containers, place equal amounts of chicken, and into the other 2 add the cubed tofu and ½ cup of edamame.

▶

¼ cup fresh or frozen yellow corn kernels

1 baby portobello mushroom, halved and cut into ¼-inch strips

1 tablespoon chopped fresh cilantro

1 tablespoon chopped scallions

Sesame seeds, for garnish (optional)

⑤ Store the airtight containers in the refrigerator for up to 4 days.

Reheat When ready to eat, add 1 to 1¼ cups of water and microwave for 2 to 3 minutes until heated through. Mix everything together in the container or dump into a bowl for easier slurping.

TIP Miso paste is often sold in a large quantity, but it's so versatile and a condiment I feel is worth having. Miso can be used in marinades, dressings, soups, and even in sweet desserts for a salty touch.

Per Serving (1 container with chicken): Calories: 589; Fat: 23g; Protein: 38g; Total Carbs: 57g; Fiber: 3g; Sodium: 1898mg; Iron: 4mg

Per Serving (1 container with tofu and edamame): Calories: 619; Fat: 28g; Protein: 27g; Total Carbs: 65g; Fiber: 6g; Sodium: 1856mg; Iron: 6mg

DIY Steak (Black Bean) Fajita Bowls

DAIRY-FREE, GLUTEN-FREE, NUT-FREE *(GLUTEN-FREE, NUT-FREE, VEGAN)*

PREP 15 min • **MARINATE** 15 min • **COOK** 20 min • **MAKES** 4 servings (2 per variety)

Mexican food is easy to customize. I recommend using instant brown rice to cut the grain cooking time in half. Two corn tortillas can also be substituted for the rice.

2 teaspoons chili powder

4 teaspoons avocado oil, divided

1 teaspoon ground cumin

½ teaspoon salt

8 ounces flank steak, cut widthwise into ½-inch strips

1 cup dried instant brown rice

1 red bell pepper, cut into ½-inch strips

1 green bell pepper, cut into ½-inch strips

1 yellow bell pepper, cut into ½-inch strips

1 large yellow onion, halved and cut into ¼-inch slices

1 (15.5-ounce) can low-sodium black beans, drained and rinsed

1 avocado, peeled, pitted, and chopped

1 lime, quartered

1 cup pico de gallo

1. Preheat the oven to 375°F.

2. In a medium bowl, whisk together the chili powder, 1 teaspoon of avocado oil, cumin, and salt. Add the sliced steak, toss to coat, and marinate for 10 to 15 minutes.

3. While the steak is marinating, prepare the rice according to the package instructions. Once cooked, set aside.

4. On a baking sheet, combine the bell peppers and onion and toss with the remaining 3 teaspoons of avocado oil. Add the steak to the baking sheet and spread everything into an even layer. Bake for 10 minutes, rotate the pan, then bake for another 10 minutes until the steak reaches an internal temperature of 165°F.

5. Into each of 4 containers, place 1 cup of pepper and onion mix and 1 cup of cooked rice. Into 2 of the containers, place equal amounts of steak, and into the other 2, place 1 cup of black beans each. Into 4 separate containers, pack a quarter of the avocado, 1 lime quarter, and ¼ cup of pico de gallo. Store in the refrigerator for up to 4 days.

🔥 **Reheat** Reheat in the microwave for 1 to 2 minutes.

❄ **Freeze** Freeze for up to 2 months. To thaw, refrigerate overnight.

Per Serving (1 container with steak): Calories: 535; Fat: 23g; Protein: 31g; Total Carbs: 53g; Fiber: 7g; Sodium: 389mg; Iron: 2mg

Per Serving (1 container with black beans): Calories: 449; Fat: 13g; Protein: 15g; Total Carbs: 72g; Fiber: 16g; Sodium: 546mg; Iron: 10mg

Citrus Lentil Grain Bowl, page 95

PREP 8

WEEKDAY WARRIORS

Welcome, warriors! This final plan has breakfasts, lunches, and dinners for two for the entire week. But not to fear, this prep is spread over two days to keep the prep easy and the meals fresh. The recipes are kept simple as well—smoothies, freezer-friendly waffles and casseroles, and easy sheet pan and stir-fry meals are included to show you how easy cooking nutritious and delicious food for two can be.

	Day	Breakfast	Lunch	Dinner
PREP DAY #1	M	Dark Chocolate Beet Smoothie	Citrus Lentil Grain Bowl	Sheet Pan Pesto Chicken and Asparagus with Gnocchi
	T	Dark Chocolate Beet Smoothie	Sheet Pan Pesto Chicken and Asparagus with Gnocchi	Sesame Green Bean Stir-Fry with Honey Shrimp
	W	Dark Chocolate Beet Smoothie	Citrus Lentil Grain Bowl	Sesame Green Bean Stir-Fry with Honey Shrimp
PREP DAY #2	TH	Superfood Blender Waffles	Grown-Up Mac and Cheese	Baja Chicken Quesadilla
	F	Superfood Blender Waffles	Baja Chicken Quesadilla	Grown-Up Mac and Cheese

SHOPPING LIST

Pantry

- [ ] Almond milk, unsweetened (18 ounces)
- [ ] Baking powder
- [ ] Cocoa powder, unsweetened
- [ ] Farro
- [ ] Flaxseed, ground
- [ ] Flour, oat
- [ ] Honey
- [ ] Lentils, black or French
- [ ] Maple syrup
- [ ] Nonstick olive oil cooking spray
- [ ] Nut butter (optional)
- [ ] Oil, olive, extra-virgin
- [ ] Pasta, dried, short cut, legume-based, 1 (8-ounce) package
- [ ] Sesame seeds
- [ ] Soy sauce, low-sodium
- [ ] Tortillas, whole-wheat, 1 (10-count) package
- [ ] Vanilla extract
- [ ] Vegetable broth, low-sodium (24 ounces)
- [ ] Vinegar, red wine
- [ ] Walnuts raw, unsalted (3 tablespoons)

Herbs and Spices

- [ ] Black pepper, whole
- [ ] Chili powder, chipotle
- [ ] Cinnamon, ground
- [ ] Garlic powder
- [ ] Red pepper flakes
- [ ] Salt

Produce

- [ ] Arugula (8 ounces)
- [ ] Asparagus (1 bunch)
- [ ] Avocados (2)
- [ ] Bananas (6)
- [ ] Beets, precooked, 2 (8.8-ounce) packages
- [ ] Blood oranges (2)
- [ ] Broccolini (1 pound)
- [ ] Butternut squash (3 pounds)
- [ ] Cilantro (1 bunch)
- [ ] Garlic (1 head)
- [ ] Ginger paste, 1 (4-ounce) tube
- [ ] Green beans (12 ounces)
- [ ] Lemon (1)
- [ ] Limes (2)
- [ ] Onion, yellow, medium (1)
- [ ] Radicchio (1 head)
- [ ] Spinach, baby, 2 (6-ounce) bags

Protein

- [ ] Chicken breast, boneless, skinless (2 pounds)
- [ ] Eggs, large (4)
- [ ] Shrimp, medium (1 pound)

Dairy

- [ ] Butter, unsalted
- [ ] Cheddar cheese, sharp, shredded (12 ounces)
- [ ] Greek yogurt, plain, 1 (16-ounce) container
- [ ] Milk, 2 percent (8 ounces)
- [ ] Monterey cheese, shredded (5 ounces)
- [ ] Parmesan cheese, grated (2 ounces)
- [ ] Yogurt, for topping (optional)

Frozen

- [ ] Gnocchi, 2 (17.5-ounce) packages
- [ ] Corn, 1 (10-ounce) bag

EQUIPMENT

- [ ] Aluminum foil
- [ ] Baking dish (9-by-7-inch)
- [ ] Blender
- [ ] Chef's knife
- [ ] Cutting board
- [ ] Immersion blender (optional)
- [ ] Measuring cups and spoons
- [ ] Mixing bowls
- [ ] Mixing spoon
- [ ] Sauce pots
- [ ] Sheet pans
- [ ] Skillet
- [ ] Slotted spoon
- [ ] Spatula
- [ ] Waffle iron
- [ ] Whisk

PREP CONTAINERS

- [ ] **Sheet Pan Pesto Chicken and Asparagus with Gnocchi:** 4 glass containers
- [ ] **Citrus Lentil Grain Bowl:** 4 containers
- [ ] **Dark Chocolate Beet Smoothie:** 6 jars or 6 resealable sandwich bags
- [ ] **Sesame Green Bean Stir-Fry with Honey Shrimp:** 4 glass containers
- [ ] **Grown-Up Mac and Cheese:** 4 glass containers
- [ ] **Superfood Blender Waffles:** 4 containers or 4 resealable sandwich bags
- [ ] **Baja Chicken Quesadilla:** 4 glass containers

STEP-BY-STEP PREP DAY #1

Sheet Pan Pesto Chicken and Asparagus with Gnocchi, page 94	**Citrus Lentil Grain Bowl,** page 95	**Dark Chocolate Beet Smoothie,** page 96	**Sesame Green Bean Stir-Fry with Honey Shrimp,** page 97

▶ **START HERE**

Prepare steps ① through ④. Once the chicken and asparagus are out of the oven, lower the temperature to 350°F, and . . . ┄┄┄┄┄▶

Prepare steps ② through ⑤. While the grains are still cooking . . .

Finish steps ⑤ ◀┄┄┄┄┄ through ⑥.

Finish steps ⑥ through ⑦.

Prepare in full. ┄┄┄┄┄▶

Prepare in full.

STEP-BY-STEP PREP DAY #2

Grown-Up Mac and Cheese, page 98	**Superfood Blender Waffles,** page 99	**Baja Chicken Quesadilla,** page 100

► START HERE

Prepare steps ① through ⑥. While the mac and cheese is in the broiler ...

Prepare steps ① through ③. While the waffles are cooling ...

Finish step ⑦.

Finish steps ④ through ⑤.

Prepare in full.

Sheet Pan Pesto Chicken and Asparagus with Gnocchi

PREP 5 minutes · COOK 20 minutes · MAKES 4 servings

Premade gnocchi is one of my favorite shortcut items. You can find it at most grocery stores nowadays, either frozen or vacuum-packed fresh. In this recipe, the chicken and asparagus are conveniently baking on the same sheet pan while you cook the gnocchi. Then everything gets tossed in a bright pesto sauce!

1 pound boneless, skinless chicken breast, cut into 4 pieces

1 bunch asparagus, spears cut into 1-inch pieces

3 tablespoons extra-virgin olive oil

½ teaspoon salt

½ teaspoon freshly ground black pepper

4 cups premade potato gnocchi

1 cup Lemon Arugula Pesto (page 149)

1. Preheat the oven to 375°F.

2. Line a sheet pan with aluminum foil and place the chicken breasts on it side by side. Scatter the asparagus around the chicken. Drizzle the olive oil, salt, and pepper over everything and toss to coat evenly. Place the sheet in the oven and bake for about 20 minutes, until the chicken has reached an internal cooking temperature of 165°F.

3. While the chicken and asparagus are cooking, fill a large pot with water for the gnocchi. Bring the water to a boil and drop in half the gnocchi. Cook the gnocchi, stirring gently, until tender, about 1 minute after they rise to the surface. Using a slotted spoon, transfer the cooked gnocchi to a large bowl. Repeat with the remaining gnocchi.

4. Prepare the Lemon Arugula Pesto.

5. Into each of 4 containers, place 1 piece of chicken, a quarter of the asparagus, and a quarter of the gnocchi. Top with the desired amount of pesto.

6. Store in airtight containers in the refrigerator for up to 4 days.

TIP If following a lower carbohydrate diet, swap the potato gnocchi for cauliflower gnochi.

Per Serving (1 container): Calories: 814; Fat: 48g; Protein: 42g; Total Carbs: 59g; Fiber: 2g; Sodium: 1030mg; Iron: 4mg

Citrus Lentil Grain Bowl

NUT-FREE, VEGAN

PREP 10 minutes • **COOK** 30 minutes • **MAKES** 4 servings

Farro has a nutty flavor and is high in fiber and iron. This grain bowl combines farro with lentils for a meatless meal that is brightened by blood oranges.

For the bowls

1 pound broccolini, stems trimmed about 2 inches

1 tablespoon extra-virgin olive oil

½ teaspoon salt

¼ teaspoon freshly ground black pepper

1 cup dried black or French lentils

5½ cups water, divided

¾ cup dried farro

4 cups arugula

1 small head radicchio, roughly chopped

2 blood oranges, peeled and cut into 1-inch cubes

1 avocado, peeled, pitted, and cut into bite-size chunks

For the dressing

2 tablespoons red wine vinegar

3 tablespoons extra-virgin olive oil

Salt

Freshly ground black pepper

1. Preheat the oven to 350°F.

2. Line a baking sheet with aluminum foil and place the broccolini on the sheet. Drizzle with the olive oil, salt, and pepper, and toss to combine. Roast for 20 minutes until the broccolini stems are tender.

3. In a pot, combine the lentils and 3 cups of water and bring to a boil over high heat. Cover, reduce the heat to a simmer, and cook until tender, about 25 minutes, adding more water as needed. Set aside.

4. In another pot, combine the farro and 2½ cups of water. Bring to a boil then reduce the heat to medium and cook until the grains are tender, about 30 minutes. Set aside.

5. To make the dressing, in a small bowl, whisk the red wine vinegar, olive oil, salt, and pepper and set aside.

6. In a large bowl, combine the broccolini, lentils, farro, arugula, radicchio, blood oranges, and avocado. Drizzle the dressing over everything and gently toss to coat.

7. Into each of 4 containers, place equal amounts of salad. Store in the refrigerator for up to 3 days.

TIP The acid from the blood oranges and vinegar dressing will help keep the avocado from browning. To eliminate the possibility of browning, you could prep this meal on the morning of the day you plan to consume it.

Per Serving (1 container): Calories: 566; Fat: 22g; Protein: 22g; Total Carbs: 73g; Fiber: 27g; Sodium: 351mg; Iron: 6mg

Dark Chocolate Beet Smoothie

GLUTEN-FREE, NUT-FREE, VEGETARIAN

PREP 10 minutes · **MAKES** 6 servings

Smoothies often get a bad rap for not being healthy, but not all smoothies are created equal. Even when making a drinkable meal, you should include protein, fat, starch, and fiber to provide ultimate satisfaction and sustained energy. Don't be scared off by the beets—with the banana and cocoa powder, you can't even taste them. Plus, beets are a great source of folate and vitamin C, and they contain nitrates that help with blood flow and athletic performance.

6 bananas, peeled and halved

3 cups cooked beets, quartered

1¾ cups plain Greek yogurt

1 cup low-fat milk or dairy-free milk

½ cup unsweetened cocoa powder

⅓ cup ground flaxseed

1½ teaspoons ground cinnamon

4 ice cubes

1. In a blender, combine the bananas, beets, yogurt, milk, cocoa powder, flaxseed, cinnamon, and ice. Blend until well combined, and add more milk to achieve your desired texture, if required. If your blender is not large enough, you may have to divide the ingredients in half and prepare in two batches.

2. Into each of 6 containers or jars, pour equal amounts of smoothie.

3. Store the airtight containers in the refrigerator for up to 4 days. Shake when ready to consume as the solids and liquid may have separated a bit.

❄ **Freeze** Freeze for up to 2 months. Thaw in the refrigerator overnight and reblend when ready to drink.

TIP You can also pre-portion ingredients and blend the morning of, if preferred. Divide the above ingredients into 6 resealable bags, leaving out the milk, and store the bags in the freezer. Thaw in the refrigerator overnight, then add the milk and blend.

Per Serving (1 container): Calories: 274; Fat: 8g; Protein: 9g; Total Carbs: 48g; Fiber: 9g; Sodium: 132mg; Iron: 4mg

Sesame Green Bean Stir-Fry with Honey Shrimp

DAIRY-FREE, NUT-FREE

PREP 10 minutes · **COOK** 15 minutes · **MAKES** 4 servings

When my partner and I haven't planned anything for dinner, stir-fry is our go-to meal. Making it yourself allows you to be in control of the ingredients, especially the salt and sugar, which are often overused in takeout restaurants. You can use freshly grated ginger and store the leftover root in the freezer, or you can pick up a tube of ginger paste that will last in your refrigerator for a few months.

1 pound medium shrimp, peeled and deveined

1 garlic clove, minced

1 teaspoon ginger paste

1 teaspoon honey

2 tablespoons extra-virgin olive oil

4 cups fresh or frozen corn kernels

4 cups chopped green beans

2 tablespoons low-sodium soy sauce

½ teaspoon red pepper flakes

½ cup chopped fresh cilantro

2 teaspoons sesame seeds

1. In a medium bowl, toss the shrimp, garlic, ginger, and honey. Set aside.

2. In a large skillet, heat the olive oil over medium heat. When the oil is shimmering, add the corn and green beans and cover. Cook for about 5 minutes, then remove the cover and stir. Add the soy sauce and red pepper flakes. Continue to cook for 3 to 4 more minutes, then transfer the corn and beans to a bowl and set aside.

3. To the hot skillet, add the marinated shrimp. Sauté for 3 to 4 minutes until cooked through and no longer pink. Return the vegetables to the skillet, add the cilantro, and stir everything together for 1 minute, adding a touch of water if needed to prevent sticking.

4. Into each of 4 containers, place equal amounts of stir-fry mixture and top each with ½ teaspoon of sesame seeds.

5. Store the airtight containers in the refrigerator for up to 4 days.

TIP Corn is a pretty starchy vegetable, but if you find you have a larger appetite, this stir-fry could be served over some brown rice.

Per Serving (1 container): Calories: 347; Fat: 11g; Protein: 31g; Total Carbs: 40g; Fiber: 8g; Sodium: 601mg; Iron: 3mg

Grown-Up Mac and Cheese

GLUTEN-FREE, NUT-FREE, VEGETARIAN

PREP 5 minutes · **COOK** 20 minutes · **MAKES** 4 servings

To keep the calories and saturated fat low, this recipe cuts down on cheese by adding butternut squash purée. I recommend trying one of the newer gluten-free, legume-based pastas on the market.

Nonstick olive oil cooking spray

8 ounces legume-based pasta (chickpeas, red lentils)

1 tablespoon extra-virgin olive oil

1 medium yellow onion, chopped

6 cups cubed butternut squash

3 cups low-sodium vegetable broth

3 cups shredded sharp cheddar cheese, divided

3 cups baby spinach

Salt

Freshly ground black pepper

(1) Preheat the broiler to high and lightly grease a 9-by-7-inch baking dish with cooking spray or butter.

(2) Bring a large pot of water to a boil and cook the pasta according to the package instructions. Drain, rinse with cold water, and set aside.

(3) In a large pot, heat the olive oil. Add the onion and sauté for about 1 minute. Add the butternut squash and vegetable broth, then cover and bring to a simmer. Cook for about 6 minutes, until the squash is easily pierced. Remove from the heat.

(4) Use an immersion blender or regular blender to blend the squash into a smooth purée, then return the purée to the pot.

(5) To the pot, add the cooked pasta, 1 cup of cheddar cheese, and the spinach. Stir to combine, then add salt and pepper.

(6) Transfer the mixture to the baking dish and sprinkle with the remaining 2 cups of shredded cheese. Place under the broiler for 7 to 8 minutes to crisp the top.

(7) Into each of 4 containers, place equal portions of pasta bake. Store in the refrigerator for up to 5 days.

 **Reheat** Reheat for 1 to 2 minutes in the microwave.

Freeze Freeze for up to 2 months. Thaw overnight.

TIP Purchase cubed butternut squash to save time.

Per Serving (1 container): Calories: 704; Fat: 33g; Protein: 32g; Total Carbs: 72g; Fiber: 7g; Sodium: 648mg; Iron: 5mg

Superfood Blender Waffles

DAIRY-FREE, GLUTEN-FREE, VEGETARIAN

PREP 5 minutes · **COOK** 15 minutes · **MAKES** 4 servings

Meal prep where you don't even have to dirty a bowl? Yes, it's real. These waffles are made in the blender for easy prep and cleanup, so there's no excuse to not make this breakfast. Spinach, which is packed with vitamin K, iron, and calcium, is what gives these waffles their other superpower. Depending on your waffle maker, the size of the finished waffle may vary, but this recipe will end up making about 8 waffles.

4 cups oat flour

2¼ cups unsweetened almond milk

2 cups baby spinach

4 large eggs

2 tablespoons ground flaxseed

2 tablespoons baking powder

1 tablespoon ground cinnamon

1 tablespoon maple syrup

2 teaspoons vanilla extract

1 teaspoon salt

Banana slices or berries, for serving (optional)

Yogurt, for serving (optional)

Nut butter, for serving (optional)

① Preheat your waffle iron and grease it if necessary.

② In a blender, combine the oat flour, almond milk, spinach, eggs, flaxseed, baking powder, cinnamon, maple syrup, vanilla, and salt. Blend on high for about 30 seconds until mixed well.

③ Drop ⅓ to ½ cup of batter into your waffle maker, close, and let cook for 3 to 4 minutes. Gently use a rubber spatula to remove the finished waffle, and repeat with the remaining batter.

④ Into each of 4 containers or resealable sandwich bags, place 2 waffles. Add the optional fruit, yogurt, or nut butter upon packing or when ready to serve.

⑤ Store in an airtight container for up to 4 days.

🔥 **Reheat** Reheat in the toaster or microwave until warmed through.

❄ **Freeze** Lay the waffles in a single layer on a baking sheet lined with parchment paper and place in the freezer for about 2 hours. When the waffles are fully frozen, place in a freezer-safe bag or container for up to 3 months.

TIP Keep the base of these waffles the same, but feel free to use other vegetables, like squash or beet purée, for fun twists.

Per Serving (2 waffles): Calories: 539; Fat: 16g; Protein: 21g; Total Carbs: 76g; Fiber: 13g; Sodium: 874mg; Iron: 9mg

Baja Chicken Quesadilla

NUT-FREE

PREP 10 minutes · **MARINATE** 10 minutes · **COOK** 20 minutes · **MAKES** 4 servings

Quesadillas are a great vehicle for squeezing in convenient, delicious nutrition. The fillings can also be customized to you and your partner's preferences without extra effort. Quesadillas are great for meal preps, as the crispy tortilla holds up well for a few days. Serve these triangles with some fresh pico de gallo, your favorite salsa, or creamy guacamole for added flavor.

1 pound boneless, skinless chicken breasts or chicken strips

Juice of 2 limes

½ teaspoon chipotle chili powder

1 teaspoon garlic powder

½ teaspoon salt

1 avocado, peeled, pitted, and cut into quarters

8 whole-wheat tortillas

2 cups baby spinach

Nonstick olive oil cooking spray

1¼ cups shredded Monterey cheese

Butter, for greasing

1. In a shallow baking dish, lay the chicken in a single layer and add the lime juice, chili powder, garlic powder, and salt. Using your hands or tongs, turn the chicken in the marinade to coat and let sit for 10 minutes.

2. While the chicken is marinating, assemble the quesadillas. In a small bowl, use a fork to mash the avocado pieces into a creamy paste. Divide this mash amongst 4 tortillas, spreading it in an even layer. On top of the avocado layer, add about ¼ cup of spinach in an even layer. Set aside.

3. Heat a large skillet over medium heat and spray it lightly with cooking spray. Place the chicken breasts in the skillet and cook for 3 to 4 minutes per side, until an internal temperature of 165°F is reached. Remove from the skillet, let cool, then slice into thin strips.

4. Divide the cooked chicken in an even layer among the 4 prepared tortillas. Sprinkle with even amounts of cheese, then place the remaining 4 tortillas on top.

⑤ Wipe the skillet clean and heat a small amount of butter over medium heat. Add 1 quesadilla to the skillet. When the tortilla is golden on the first side, carefully flip it to the other side, adding another touch of butter to the skillet as needed. Continue cooking until the second side is golden. Repeat with the remaining quesadillas. Cut the quesadillas into quarters.

⑥ Into each of 4 containers, place 4 quesadilla triangles with any desired toppings. Store in airtight containers in the refrigerator for up to 3 days.

🔥 **Reheat** Warm in a toaster oven until heated through or microwave for 1 to 2 minutes.

❄️ **Freeze** Place individual quesadillas on a baking sheet lined with parchment paper and freeze them for 1 to 2 hours, until frozen. Remove them from the baking sheet and place them inside a freezer-safe bag or container.

TIP Feel free to add in more Baja California–inspired veggies like peppers, onions, or tomatoes, or swap the chicken for mashed pinto or black beans.

Per Serving (1 quesadilla): Calories: 509; Fat: 26g; Protein: 36g; Total Carbs: 32g; Fiber: 7g; Sodium: 778mg; Iron: 1mg

PART TWO

MEAL PREP RECIPES *for* TWO

I N THIS SECTION you'll find additional recipes for breakfasts, lunches, and dinners as well as for staple sauces and pantry items and snacks. These recipes can become the foundation for building your own meal preps, or they can easily be swapped into any of the outlined plans in this book.

Here are some considerations for recipe swaps:

Prep and cooking time: If you want to change a 10-minute snack for something that takes more hands-on time to prepare, determine whether your prep day allows for the additional steps. Alternatively, if you expect a busy week, choose a slow cooker meal to replace one that requires more stove time.

Use of easily substitutable ingredients: Can't find or don't like one kind of veggie? Use another. Have a lot of one veggie? Make it the week's theme. If you can find only a very large butternut squash, for example, try making the week "Butternut Week." Prepare the Grown-Up Mac and Cheese (page 98) and substitute the acorn squash with the butternut squash in the Rosemary Chicken with Maple-Roasted Winter Squash (page 136). Swap one fresh herb for another if need or taste dictates.

Vegetarian/vegan needs: Many of the recipes in this book accommodate both meat eaters and vegetarians/vegans, but not all of them. Be mindful of whether a recipe allows for protein substitutions.

*Zucchini Cheddar
Scones,* page 110

BREAKFASTS

Pineapple Ginger Parfait

GLUTEN-FREE, VEGETARIAN

PREP 10 minutes • **MAKES** 6 servings

These cheery mason jar breakfasts transport me to a Hawaiian island. This breakfast is packed with pineapple, which is high in vitamin C and bromelain, a protein-digesting enzyme that can help with inflammation and swelling. Feel free to customize these ginger-scented fruit parfaits. I think a plum-and-ginger combination is divine.

6 cups plain Greek yogurt

2 tablespoons grated fresh ginger

1 tablespoon honey

6 cups chopped pineapple

½ cup sliced almonds

1. In a medium bowl, combine the yogurt, ginger, and honey and stir to combine.

2. Into each of 6 containers, place 1 cup of pineapple at the bottom, then top with 1 cup of yogurt mixture and a sprinkle of chopped almonds.

3. Store the airtight containers in the refrigerator for up to 5 days.

TIP The yogurt could easily be replaced by a layer of easy chia pudding. Follow step 1 for the Tropical Chia Pudding (page 24) and add this on top of the pineapple instead.

Per Serving (1 container): Calories: 225; Fat: 4g; Protein: 18g; Total Carbs: 34g; Fiber: 4g; Sodium: 63mg; Iron: 2mg

Apple Nut Butter Quesadilla

VEGAN

PREP 10 minutes · **MAKES** 4 servings

No longer are quesadillas reserved for savory preparations. Most people find it easiest to consume a serving of fruit in the morning, so this sweet quesadilla calls for apple slices (berries and banana would also work well) sandwiched in a whole-wheat tortilla for maximum portability and meal prep functionality. The fruit is paired with protein and healthy fats for a satisfying breakfast.

Per quesadilla (x4)

- 2 whole-wheat tortillas, divided
- 2 tablespoons almond butter, smooth or crunchy
- ½ apple, cut into ¼-inch slices
- 1 tablespoon hemp seeds
- Pinch ground cinnamon

1. Lay 1 tortilla on a cutting board and spread the almond butter onto the base. Place the apple slices onto the almond butter, then sprinkle with the hemp seeds and cinnamon. Place the remaining tortilla on top, press down lightly, and cut into quarters. Repeat to create 3 additional quesadillas.

2. Into each of 4 containers, place 1 quartered quesadilla.

3. Store the airtight containers in the refrigerator for up to 3 days.

TIP Feel free to eat these quesadillas cold, or, when ready to serve, you can warm them on a lightly buttered griddle for extra crispiness.

Per Serving (1 quesadilla): Calories: 457; Fat: 26g; Protein: 17g; Total Carbs: 45g; Fiber: 11g; Sodium: 461mg; Iron: 4mg

Chocolate Cherry Oatmeal Cups

VEGAN

PREP 10 minutes · **COOK** 35 minutes · **MAKES** 12 muffins

It might not be scientifically proven, but I believe couples who have chocolate for breakfast are happier than couples who don't. To start your day off right, prep a batch of these oat cups, which contain ample fiber, protein, and a rich chocolate flavor. Unsweetened cocoa powder is an excellent pantry staple to use for breakfasts, snacks, and healthier desserts.

Nonstick olive oil cooking spray

3 cups old-fashioned oats

¼ cup plus 1 tablespoon unsweetened cocoa powder

¼ cup chocolate protein powder

1 teaspoon baking powder

½ teaspoon salt

2 cups almond milk

2 cups halved cherries

2 large eggs, beaten

2 tablespoons coconut oil

2 tablespoons maple syrup

1. Preheat the oven to 375°F. Coat a 12-cup muffin tin with cooking spray.

2. In a large bowl, combine the oats, cocoa powder, protein powder, baking powder, and salt. Mix well. Add in the almond milk, cherries, eggs, coconut oil, and maple syrup. Stir together until well combined.

3. Scoop the mixture evenly into the muffin tin and bake for 30 to 35 minutes, until a toothpick inserted into the center of a muffin comes out clean. Remove the muffins from the cups and allow to cool before storing.

4. Into each of 6 containers or eco-friendly sandwich bags, place 2 muffins.

5. Store the airtight containers in the refrigerator for up to 5 days.

 Reheat Warm in the microwave for 1 minute.

❄ **Freeze** Freeze for up to 2 months.

TIP If you don't want to use protein powder, you can simply omit or toss in some hemp seeds or sliced almonds for a protein source. A yogurt topping is also a nice protein addition.

Per Serving (2 muffins): Calories: 156; Fat: 6g; Protein: 7g; Total Carbs: 21g; Fiber: 3g; Sodium: 185mg; Iron: 2mg

Blueberry Fool Overnight Oats

GLUTEN-FREE

PREP 5 minutes · MAKES 8 servings

Do you know what a *fool* is? It's an English dessert that folds cooked fruit into a sugary whipped cream base. Blueberry fool was my favorite childhood dessert, so I've turned it into a lightened-up breakfast perfect for meal prep.

Per container (x8)

1 cup unsweetened dairy-free milk (soy, almond, oat)

½ cup old-fashioned oats

Pinch salt

1 tablespoon plain yogurt (regular or Greek)

½ teaspoon grated lemon zest (4 teaspoons total)

¼ cup Blueberry Chia Jam (page 150) (2 cups total)

1. Gather 8 (16-ounce) jars or other prep containers. Into each jar, place the dairy-free milk, oats, and salt. Give this a quick stir.

2. Then add in the yogurt, lemon zest, and Blueberry Chia Jam. Cover and place the jars in the refrigerator.

3. Store the airtight containers in the refrigerator for up to 5 days.

Per Serving (1 container): Calories: 300; Fat: 11g; Protein: 11g; Total Carbs: 40g; Fiber: 8g; Sodium: 528mg; Iron: 5mg

Zucchini Cheddar Scones

PREP 15 minutes · **COOK** 25 minutes · **MAKES** 8 scones

Breads and scones make great meal preps for busy couples. The trick with these zucchini scones is making sure to squeeze out the excess water from the shredded zucchini to avoid soggy scones. While you prepare the dough, let the zucchini sit in a strainer and then give it a good squeeze or press it in a cheesecloth to remove the liquid.

2½ cups all-purpose flour, plus 1 tablespoon

¼ cup granulated sugar

1½ teaspoons baking powder

1 teaspoon salt

1 teaspoon dried thyme

½ teaspoon baking soda

8 tablespoons (1 stick) cold unsalted butter, cut into very small pieces

¾ cup low-fat milk

1 large egg

2 teaspoons white vinegar or lemon juice

1 cup shredded zucchini

1 cup shredded cheddar cheese, divided

1. Preheat the oven to 400°F. Line two baking sheets with parchment paper and set aside.

2. In a large bowl, combine 2½ cups of flour, the sugar, baking powder, salt, thyme, and baking soda and stir to combine.

3. Add the butter to the bowl and, using your hands, quickly work the butter into the flour mixture until it resembles a coarse meal.

4. In a small bowl, combine the milk, egg, and vinegar, then add this to the flour and butter mixture.

5. In a separate bowl, combine the shredded zucchini, ¾ cup of cheddar cheese, and the remaining 1 tablespoon of flour. Toss to coat, then add this zucchini mixture to the dough and combine gently.

6. Pour the dough out onto a clean, lightly floured surface and gently work it into a round mound. Press it out into an 8-inch circle that is about ½ inch thick. Cut it into 8 triangles and transfer each triangle to the lined baking sheets. Sprinkle the remaining ¼ cup of cheddar cheese on top of the scones.

7. Bake for 20 to 25 minutes, or until the tops of the scones are a golden brown and a toothpick inserted in a scone comes out clean.

8. Store in airtight containers in the refrigerator for up to 3 days.

Reheat If you'd prefer your scone to be warm, reheat in the microwave for 30 seconds or toaster oven for 1 minute.

Freeze Freeze for up to 3 months. To reheat, bake in a 300°F oven for 20 minutes until warmed.

Per Serving (1 scone): Calories: 355; Fat: 17g; Protein: 11g; Total Carbs: 40g; Fiber: 3g; Sodium: 561mg; Iron: 3mg

Good Morning Sweet Potato Jacket

GLUTEN-FREE OPTION, VEGETARIAN

PREP 5 minutes · **COOK** 15 minutes · **MAKES** 4 servings

Have you ever made something to eat and your partner gave you the what-the-heck-is-that look? Breakfast sweet potatoes puzzled my husband until he tried them. Simply cook a potato in the microwave (or oven if you have the time), and you can each customize the toppings to your liking. Here's one example.

Per sweet potato jacket (x4)

1 small sweet potato

½ cup plain yogurt

2 tablespoons almond butter

3 tablespoons granola

1. Pierce each sweet potato several times with a fork and cook the sweet potatoes in the microwave until tender and the flesh is pierced easily with a fork, about 15 minutes. Let cool, then wrap each cooked potato in aluminum foil or store in a container or eco-friendly bag.

2. In a small container, combine the yogurt, almond butter, and granola and store separately.

3. Store the airtight containers in the refrigerator for up to 3 days.

🔥 **Reheat** Warm the potato in the microwave for 1 to 2 minutes, then top with the cold yogurt cup.

TIP Store-bought granola can be heavy on the sugar. Check the nutrition facts label and aim for a granola that has 10 grams of sugar, or less, per half-cup serving. If you wish to make this dish gluten-free, be sure to look for a gluten-free granola.

Per Serving (1 potato with toppings): Calories: 426; Fat: 23g; Protein: 14g; Total Carbs: 45g; Fiber: 8g; Sodium: 135mg; Iron: 7mg

Strawberry Balsamic French Toast Bake

NUT-FREE, VEGETARIAN

PREP 10 minutes · **CHILL** 1 hour · **COOK** 40 minutes · **MAKES** 6 servings

Why wait for the weekend to have French toast? This baked version allows you to enjoy it all week. For this recipe, stale bread works best because it soaks up the custard well.

Unsalted butter, for greasing

8 (1-inch-thick) slices brioche bread (stale or oven-dried), cut into 1-inch cubes, divided

4 ounces mascarpone

2 tablespoons powdered sugar

1 teaspoon vanilla extract

2 cups sliced or chopped strawberries, divided

4 large eggs

1 cup whole milk

⅓ cup brown sugar

2 tablespoons balsamic vinegar, plus more for serving

1. Grease an 8-by-12-inch baking dish with butter or cooking spray. Place half of the cubed bread into the dish.

2. In a small bowl, mix together the mascarpone, powdered sugar, and vanilla until smooth. Using a spoon, dollop this mixture on top of the bread and spread it out. Top with 1 cup of strawberries, then the remaining cubed bread, and finish with the remaining 1 cup of strawberries.

3. In a large bowl, whisk together the eggs, milk, brown sugar, and balsamic vinegar. Pour this mixture evenly over the bread. Use the back of a spatula to gently push the mixture down so that the top layer of bread soaks up some of the custard. Cover with aluminum foil or plastic wrap and let sit in the refrigerator for at least 1 hour.

4. Preheat the oven to 350°F. Remove the foil and bake the French toast bake for 30 to 40 minutes, until the top begins to brown. Remove, let cool, and divide into 6 equal squares. Drizzle with additional balsamic, if desired.

5. Into each of 6 containers, place 1 square. Store in the refrigerator for up to 4 days.

 **Reheat** Reheat in the microwave for 45 seconds.

Freeze This bake can be frozen at step 3. Cover tightly with a lid or aluminum foil and store in the freezer for up to 2 months. To thaw, refrigerate overnight. Warm in a 350°F oven for about 25 minutes.

Per Serving (1 square): Calories: 397; Fat: 23g; Protein: 9g; Total Carbs: 37g; Fiber: 2g; Sodium: 77mg; Iron: 1mg

Pumpkin Pancakes

DAIRY-FREE OPTION, NUT-FREE, VEGETARIAN

PREP 10 minutes · **COOK** 25 minutes · **MAKES** 8 servings

Like the Superfood Blender Waffles (page 99), these autumn-inspired pancakes can be blended up and griddled in no time, making them an easy win for meal prep day. Pumpkin pairs quite nicely with other warm and toasty flavors, which is why I recommend using buckwheat flour. It's easy enough to find in most supermarkets these days, but feel free to use whole-wheat or oat flour if your stores don't carry buckwheat.

2 cups buckwheat flour

2 cups canned pumpkin purée

2 cups low-fat milk or dairy-free milk

4 large eggs

¼ cup maple syrup

2 tablespoons melted coconut oil

2 teaspoons vanilla extract

2 tablespoons freshly squeezed lemon juice

1 teaspoon baking soda

1 teaspoon ground cinnamon

½ teaspoon ground nutmeg

Butter, for greasing

Maple syrup, for serving (optional)

Nut butter, for serving (optional)

Plain yogurt, for serving (optional)

Apple compote, for serving (optional)

1. In a blender, combine the buckwheat flour, pumpkin purée, milk, eggs, maple syrup, coconut oil, vanilla, lemon juice, baking soda, cinnamon, and nutmeg. Blend on high for about 30 seconds or until mixed well. If your blender does not have the capacity to hold all the ingredients, whisk the ingredients in a large bowl.

2. Heat a nonstick skillet over medium heat and add a small amount of butter to grease the pan. Drop ⅓ cup of batter onto the pan and cook until the edges start to puff up and look dry and the underside is lightly browned. Flip and cook for 30 to 60 more seconds. Repeat with the remaining batter.

3. If desired, serve with maple syrup, nut butter, yogurt, and/or apple compote. Store in airtight containers in the refrigerator for up to 3 days.

Reheat Warm in the microwave for 30 to 45 seconds or in a toaster oven or oven until warmed through.

Freeze Lay cooled pancakes in an even layer on a sheet pan and place them in the freezer for an hour. Remove and place in a resealable plastic bag or container, and store for up to 2 months.

Per Serving (3 pancakes): Calories: 321; Fat: 14g; Protein: 12g; Total Carbs: 38g; Fiber: 9g; Sodium: 266mg; Iron: 3mg

Mushroom Asparagus Quiche with Quinoa Crust

GLUTEN-FREE, NUT-FREE, VEGETARIAN

PREP 10 minutes · **COOK** 1 hour and 25 minutes · **MAKES** 8 servings

For a breakfast that goes the distance, consider a quiche. By combining eggs, cheese, and vegetables, you get a balanced breakfast that's sure to satisfy you all week long. Fun fact: Mushrooms are the only item in the produce aisle that contain vitamin D. The crust for this recipe is gluten-free because it uses quinoa. It's an extra step, but quite worth it if you or your partner have an allergy or sensitivity.

For the quinoa

1½ cups water

½ cup uncooked quinoa

1 tablespoon extra-virgin olive oil

For the crust

2 large eggs

½ cup grated Parmesan cheese

2 teaspoons garlic powder

2 teaspoons onion powder

1 teaspoon dried thyme

For the filling

2 tablespoons extra-virgin olive oil, divided

1 shallot, chopped

2 cups chopped asparagus

3 cups chopped cremini mushrooms

6 large eggs, beaten

1 cup crumbled goat cheese

1 teaspoon salt

½ teaspoon freshly ground black pepper

1. Preheat the oven to 375°F.

2. To make the quinoa, in a medium sauce pot, bring the water, quinoa, and olive oil to a boil over high heat. Reduce the heat to a simmer, cover, and let cook until most of the water has been absorbed, about 15 minutes. Remove from the heat and let sit, covered, for 5 minutes. Fluff the quinoa with a fork and cool to room temperature.

3. To make the crust, in a large bowl, combine the eggs, Parmesan, garlic powder, onion powder, and thyme. Stir in the cooled quinoa.

4. Spread the crust mixture into an 11-inch tart pan or pie dish, pressing it into the bottom and up the sides to create the crust edge. Bake for 15 minutes, until lightly browned. Remove and let cool 5 minutes.

5. To make the filling, in a medium skillet, heat 1 tablespoon of olive oil over medium heat. When the oil is shimmering, add the shallot and sauté for 2 to 3 minutes. Toss in the asparagus and cook for 5 minutes. Add in the mushrooms and the remaining 1 tablespoon of olive oil. Sauté everything for another 5 to 7 minutes, until the asparagus has browned and the mushrooms have softened. Remove from the heat.

▶

⑥ In a large bowl, combine the cooked vegetables with the beaten eggs, goat cheese, salt, and pepper. Pour this mixture into the prepared quinoa crust. Bake for 35 to 40 minutes until golden brown and set in the center.

⑦ Remove the finished quiche from the oven, let cool, and divide into 8 slices. Into each of 8 containers, place 1 slice of quiche. Store the airtight containers in the refrigerator for up to 4 days.

Reheat Warm in the microwave for 30 to 45 seconds or in a toaster oven or oven until warmed through.

Freeze Freeze for up to 2 months. To thaw, refrigerate overnight.

Per Serving (1 slice): Calories: 238; Fat: 15g; Protein: 14g; Total Carbs: 12g; Fiber: 2g; Sodium: 487mg; Iron: 2mg

Italian Sausage Breakfast Bake

NUT-FREE

PREP 20 minutes · **COOK** 55 minutes · **MAKES** 6 servings

Breakfast meat plus eggs plus Italian seasonings—what's not to love? This breakfast bake is a take on a strata or savory bread pudding. Keep this meal heart healthy by substituting chicken or turkey sausage or simply skip the added protein altogether and pile on more veggies, such as mushrooms.

Nonstick olive oil
  cooking spray

3 cups cubed Italian bread

¾ pound ground pork
  sausage, removed
  from casings

1 yellow bell pepper, chopped

1 red bell pepper, chopped

½ large yellow onion,
  thinly sliced

2 cups baby spinach

6 large eggs

1 cup low-fat milk

½ teaspoon fennel seed

½ teaspoon dried rosemary

¼ teaspoon freshly ground
  black pepper

¼ teaspoon salt

① Preheat the oven to 400°F. Spray a 9-by-13-inch baking dish with cooking spray and set aside.

② Lay the cubed bread on a baking sheet and coat with a light layer of cooking spray. Bake until the cubes begin to turn golden brown, 10 to 12 minutes. Remove from the oven and set aside in a large bowl.

③ Heat a medium skillet over high heat and spray lightly with cooking spray. Add the sausage and break it up, using a wooden spoon, until cooked through, 5 to 7 minutes. Transfer the sausage to the bread bowl.

④ To the heated skillet, add the bell peppers and onion and cook for 7 to 8 minutes, until the onion starts to soften. At the end, add in the spinach so that it slightly wilts. Add this mixture to the bread and sausage bowl and mix to combine. Transfer the mixture to the prepared baking dish.

⑤ In a small bowl, combine the eggs, milk, fennel, rosemary, pepper, and salt. Whisk the mixture well, and pour it over the baking dish. Use a spatula to gently press the mixture down.

▶

6. Bake for 30 to 35 minutes until the liquid is set and the edges are bubbly. Remove from the oven, let cool, and cut into 6 squares.

7. Into each of 6 containers, place 1 baked square. Store in the refrigerator for up to 4 days.

Reheat Warm in the microwave for 1 to 2 minutes, or reheat in a 350°F oven for 15 minutes.

Freeze Freeze for 2 to 3 months. To thaw, refrigerate overnight.

Per Serving (1 square): Calories: 265; Fat: 9g; Protein: 23g; Total Carbs: 24g; Fiber: 2g; Sodium: 410mg; Iron: 3mg

*Grilled Persian Kebabs
over Cauliflower Rice
and Israeli Couscous,*
page 138

LUNCHES AND DINNERS

Smashed Chickpea Cobb Sandwich

NUT-FREE, VEGETARIAN

PREP 20 minutes · **MAKES** 6 servings

Sandwiches are a classic meal prep lunch, but many vegetarians feel stuck with "veggies only" options. Adding a satisfying source of protein, such as chickpeas, and healthy fats, such as avocado and tahini, will provide nutrition and flavor. This recipe is sure to be your household's new favorite vegetarian sammie.

2 (15-ounce) cans low-sodium chickpeas, drained and rinsed

1 medium avocado, peeled, pitted, and chopped (about 1 cup cubed)

1 cup quartered cherry tomatoes

¾ cup crumbled gorgonzola cheese

½ cup diced red onion

½ cup lightly packed chopped fresh parsley

2 tablespoons tahini

2 tablespoons freshly squeezed lemon juice

2 teaspoons red wine vinegar

¼ teaspoon salt

Freshly ground black pepper

12 slices whole-wheat bread

3 cups baby spinach

1. In a large bowl, combine the chickpeas and avocado. Use the back of a fork to mash these two ingredients together, leaving behind some semi-intact chickpeas.

2. Add the tomatoes, gorgonzola, red onion, parsley, tahini, lemon juice, red wine vinegar, salt, and black pepper. Use a spoon to mix everything together.

3. Into each of 6 containers, divide this mixture equally. Store 2 slices of bread and ½ cup of spinach in separate containers or sandwich bags to go with each portion.

4. Store the airtight containers in the refrigerator for up to 3 days.

Serve Create a sandwich by layering the spinach onto a slice of the bread, scooping the smashed chickpea salad on top, and topping with the remaining slice of bread.

TIP Pair this sandwich with a crisp apple or pear for a more filling lunch.

Per Serving (1 sandwich): Calories: 440; Fat: 17g; Protein: 22g; Total Carbs: 54g; Fiber: 14g; Sodium: 659mg; Iron: 5mg

Vietnamese Chicken Lettuce Wraps

DAIRY-FREE

PREP 20 minutes • **COOK** 15 minutes • **MAKES** 6 servings

A dish that gets better with time is perfect for meal prep. The flavor of these lettuce wraps gets stronger the longer the chicken mixture soaks up the marinade. Serve the noodles and chicken in pita pockets if you prefer.

6 ounces rice noodles

2 tablespoons extra-virgin olive oil

1¾ pounds boneless, skinless chicken breast, finely chopped

¼ cup chopped red onion

¼ cup chopped fresh cilantro

¼ cup low-sodium soy sauce

¼ cup fish sauce

3 tablespoons freshly squeezed lime juice

2 lemongrass stalks, white part only, finely chopped

3 garlic cloves, minced

2 tablespoons granulated sugar

1 teaspoon freshly ground black pepper

½ teaspoon ground cayenne

12 lettuce leaves

Chopped fresh cilantro, for garnish (optional)

Peanuts, for garnish (optional)

Scallions, for garnish (optional)

1. Bring a large pot of water to a boil and prepare the noodles according to the package instructions. Rinse with cold water and set aside.

2. In a large skillet, heat the olive oil over medium heat. When the oil is shimmering, add the chicken and sauté until the chicken is opaque and cooked through, about 10 minutes.

3. In a large bowl, combine the red onion, cilantro, soy sauce, fish sauce, lime juice, lemongrass, garlic, sugar, pepper, and cayenne.

4. Using a slotted spoon, transfer the cooked chicken to the bowl and combine well.

5. Into each of 6 containers, place equal amounts of chicken mixture and cooked rice noodles. Store 2 lettuce leaves separately, along with your desired toppings. When ready to serve, assemble a bit of the noodles, chicken, and toppings (if using) into each lettuce leaf and serve cold.

6. Store the airtight containers in the refrigerator for up to 4 days.

TIP If you're pressed for time or not feeling confident in your knife skills, you can use ground chicken instead of chopping up the chicken breasts.

Per Serving (1 container): Calories: 324; Fat: 8g; Protein: 30g; Total Carbs: 31g; Fiber: 1g; Sodium: 1633mg; Iron: 1mg

Lemon Shrimp Skewer Bowls

GLUTEN-FREE, NUT-FREE

PREP 15 minutes · **MARINATE** 1 hour · **COOK** 20 minutes · **MAKES** 6 servings

Salad bowls that can be enjoyed warm or cold are ideal for meal preps! For this recipe, you can sear the shrimp in a cast iron skillet rather than grilling them, or substitute thick-cut cubes of chicken breast.

For the skewers

¾ cup freshly squeezed lemon juice (about 3 lemons)

¾ cup extra-virgin olive oil

2 garlic cloves, finely chopped

1½ teaspoons kosher salt

1 teaspoon dried oregano

½ teaspoon dried basil

¼ teaspoon freshly ground black pepper

1¾ pounds large shrimp, raw, peeled and deveined, with tails removed

For the salad

3 cups quinoa

6 cups water

6 cups arugula

6 Persian cucumbers, halved lengthwise and cut into half-moon pieces

1 pint halved cherry tomatoes

1 cup crumbled feta cheese

½ red onion, thinly sliced

1. In a medium bowl, whisk together the lemon juice, olive oil, garlic, salt, oregano, basil, and pepper. Transfer about ⅓ cup of the mixture to a small bowl for later. Add the shrimp to the remaining marinade and let sit for 1 hour.

2. Soak 6 (10- or 12-inch) wooden skewers in water for about 20 minutes.

3. In a large sauce pot, combine the quinoa and water. Bring to a boil, cover, reduce the heat to medium low, and simmer until the water is absorbed, about 15 minutes. Turn off the heat and let sit for 5 minutes. Uncover, fluff the quinoa with a fork, then set aside.

4. Preheat the grill to medium-high heat.

5. Drain the shrimp from the marinade and thread onto the skewers. Grill, turning once, until the shrimp are lightly charred and cooked through, about 5 minutes. Alternatively, cook them in a skillet over medium heat for 3 minutes per side.

6. Into each of 6 containers, place ¾ cup of cooked quinoa, 1 cup of arugula, and even amounts of shrimp, cucumbers, tomatoes, feta, and onions. Drizzle 2 teaspoons of the reserved dressing over each bowl. Store in the refrigerator for up to 5 days.

 Reheat Warm in the microwave for up to 1 minute.

Per Serving (1 container): Calories: 556; Fat: 17g; Protein: 41g; Total Carbs: 64g; Fiber: 7g; Sodium: 582mg; Iron: 5mg

Spicy Korean Cod with Crunchy Cabbage Slaw

DAIRY-FREE, NUT-FREE

PREP 10 minutes · **MARINATE** 30 minutes · **COOK** 15 minutes · **MAKES** 4 servings

Looking to spice up your meal prep? This recipe utilizes spicy gochujang, a red chili paste from Korea that can be found at most supermarkets. Condiments like this are great investments for meal prep. Buy a premade slaw mix to save time and avoid potential food waste.

For the fish

1 tablespoon gochujang

1 teaspoon honey

2 teaspoons toasted sesame oil

½ teaspoon white miso paste

2 teaspoons rice wine vinegar

4 (5-ounce) cod fillets

For the slaw

3 tablespoons avocado oil

2 tablespoons rice wine vinegar

2 tablespoons toasted sesame seeds

1 tablespoon white miso paste

1 tablespoon soy sauce

2 teaspoons mayonnaise

1 garlic clove, minced

1 teaspoon grated fresh ginger

½ teaspoon sriracha

½ teaspoon honey

8 cups rainbow slaw mix (shredded cabbage and carrots)

1. Preheat the broiler.

2. In a medium, shallow container, whisk the gochujang, honey, sesame oil, miso, and rice wine vinegar. Place the cod in the dish and coat them completely. Move the fish to the refrigerator to marinate for 30 minutes.

3. To make the slaw dressing, in a small bowl, add the avocado oil, rice wine vinegar, sesame seeds, miso, soy sauce, mayonnaise, garlic, ginger, sriracha, and honey. Mix well and divide the dressing into 4 small containers.

4. Remove the fish from the refrigerator and place on a lined baking sheet. Set the sheet under the broiler and cook for 10 to 12 minutes, until the fish flakes with a fork.

5. Into each of 4 containers, place 1 cod fillet and 2 cups of rainbow slaw. Store in the refrigerator for up to 3 days. Add dressing to the slaw when ready to eat.

Reheat Warm the cod separately in the microwave or under the broiler for 1 to 2 minutes.

TIP If one or both of you have a large appetite, add some brown rice or soba noodles.

Per Serving (1 container): Calories: 336; Fat: 18g; Protein: 29g; Total Carbs: 17g; Fiber: 5g; Sodium: 610mg; Iron: 1mg

Tex-Mex Tortilla Soup

DAIRY-FREE, GLUTEN-FREE, NUT-FREE, VEGETARIAN

PREP 10 minutes · **COOK** 4 hours · **MAKES** 6 servings

Another hands-off slow cooker recipe for the win. This tortilla soup is kept vegetarian and uses beans for a high-fiber, high-iron protein source; however, shredded chicken or pork could easily be swapped in, even right before portioning into containers, if you or your partner prefer.

3 (14.5-ounce) cans fire-roasted tomatoes

4 cups vegetable broth

2 (15.5-ounce) cans low-sodium black beans, drained and rinsed

3 cups frozen corn

2 green bell peppers, chopped

1 red bell pepper, chopped

1 medium yellow onion, chopped

3 tablespoons tomato paste

1 tablespoon ground cumin

1 tablespoon chili powder

⅓ cup crumbled cotija cheese or shredded Monterey

36 thinly sliced fresh corn tortilla strips or tortilla chips, for garnish

Cilantro, for garnish

Sliced radishes, for garnish

Lime wedge, for garnish

1. In the slow cooker, combine the tomatoes and their juices, broth, beans, corn, bell peppers, onion, and tomato paste. Stir in the cumin and chili powder. Cover and cook on high for 3 to 4 hours. Taste, adjust the seasoning, and add more liquid to thin as desired.

2. Into each of 6 containers, ladle equal portions of soup and top with 6 tablespoons of cheese and 6 fried tortilla strips. For each portion, pack any additional toppings in a separate container and add when ready to serve.

3. Store the airtight containers in the refrigerator for up to 5 days.

Reheat Warm in the microwave for 1 to 2 minutes or on the stovetop.

Freeze Freeze for up to 3 months. To thaw, refrigerate overnight.

Per Serving (1 container): Calories: 263; Fat: 4g; Protein: 12g; Total Carbs: 47g; Fiber: 12g; Sodium: 763mg; Iron: 8mg

Tuna Burger with Sun-Dried Tomato Tapenade

DAIRY-FREE, NUT-FREE

PREP 15 minutes · **COOK** 10 minutes · **MAKES** 6 servings

Not everyone is a fan of canned tuna, but put it in burger form and you're likely to win over some tuna haters. Plus, these burgers are topped with a salty and zesty tapenade to which it's hard to say no. I recommend grating the carrot yourself rather than using preshredded carrots because the softer texture will mix better with the other ingredients.

3 (5-ounce) cans no-salt-added, water-packed tuna, drained

¾ cup shredded carrot

⅔ cup panko bread crumbs

⅓ cup chopped red onion

3 large eggs, beaten

1 teaspoon grated lemon zest

Nonstick olive oil cooking spray

6 English muffins, split

2 cups baby arugula

1 tomato, cut into 6 slices

½ cup Sun-Dried Tomato Tapenade (page 147)

1. In a medium bowl, combine the tuna, carrot, bread crumbs, red onion, eggs, and lemon zest. Mix well, then form into 6 equal-size patties.

2. Heat a skillet over medium heat and spray with cooking spray. Cook the burgers for 2 to 3 minutes per side.

3. In each of 6 containers, assemble a burger by placing 1 tuna burger on an English muffin base, topping it with a small handful of arugula, 1 tomato slice, and about a tablespoon of tapenade, and placing the other English muffin half on top. Alternatively, keep the English muffin separate in a sandwich bag and build the burger when ready to eat.

4. Store the airtight containers in the refrigerator for up to 3 days.

Reheat If desired, warm the tuna burger patty separately in the microwave for up to 1 minute.

Freeze To freeze the tuna burgers, wrap them individually in plastic wrap or store in freezer-safe containers for up to 2 months.

TIP These burgers would also work well with canned salmon.

Per Serving (1 complete burger): Calories: 325; Fat: 6g; Protein: 31g; Total Carbs: 37g; Fiber: 5g; Sodium: 463mg; Iron: 5mg

Fall Harvest Bowl

NUT-FREE, VEGAN

PREP 15 minutes · **COOK** 45 minutes · **MAKES** 4 servings

Sheet pans of vegetables save the day when it comes to meal prep, as you can prepare other components of a meal while the veggies roast to crispy perfection. Feel free to use other autumn root vegetables like parsnips, turnips, or carrots in this recipe as well. This bowl is vegan by design, but roasted chicken thighs would work well if you or your partner prefers.

For the bowl

1¾ pounds Brussels sprouts, halved (quartered if very large)

1½ pounds cauliflower (about 3 cups florets)

¼ cup extra-virgin olive oil, divided

1 teaspoon salt, divided

½ teaspoon freshly ground black pepper, divided

1 cup uncooked pearled barley

2½ cups water

4 cups baby arugula

1 (15.5-ounce) can lentils, drained and rinsed

¼ cup shelled pumpkin seeds (pepitas)

For the dressing

1 tablespoon Dijon mustard

1 tablespoon maple syrup

2 tablespoons balsamic vinegar

¼ cup extra-virgin olive oil

① Preheat the oven to 375°F and line two sheet pans with parchment paper.

② Place the Brussels sprouts onto one pan and the cauliflower onto the other. Add half of the olive oil, salt, and pepper over each sheet. Toss to coat well. Roast for 25 to 30 minutes, until golden brown.

③ While the vegetables are roasting, in a large pot, bring the barley and water to a boil. Reduce the heat to a simmer and cook until all of the liquid has been absorbed and the grains are tender, 40 to 45 minutes.

④ To make the dressing, whisk together the Dijon mustard, maple syrup, balsamic vinegar, and olive oil in a small bowl.

⑤ Into each of 4 containers, place 1 cup of arugula, about ⅓ cup of lentils, even amounts of Brussels sprouts and cauliflower, equal portions of cooked barley, and a tablespoon of pumpkin seeds. Into each of 4 small containers, place 2 tablespoons of dressing. Store containers in the refrigerator for up to 3 days.

🔥 **Reheat** If desired, reheat the harvest bowls in the microwave for 1 minute until just warm.

TIP Save time by using quick-cooking pearled barley, ready in just 10 minutes.

Per Serving (1 container): Calories: 667; Fat: 31g; Protein: 24g; Total Carbs: 87g; Fiber: 26g; Sodium: 740mg; Iron: 9mg

Skillet Zucchini Lasagna

NUT-FREE, VEGETARIAN

PREP 10 minutes · **COOK** 40 minutes · **MAKES** 6 servings

Lasagna is a crowd-pleaser, but boiling noodles and layering them one by one is something most busy couples don't have time for. Instead, pick up some no-boil noodles and whip up this skillet version in no time. Plus, the tofu in this dish will have any meat-lover fooled.

1½ cups ricotta cheese

1 cup silken tofu

2 teaspoons dried oregano

1 teaspoon red pepper flakes

1 teaspoon salt

3 tablespoons extra-virgin olive oil

1 medium onion, chopped

3 medium zucchini, halved lengthwise and cut into ¼-inch slices

5 garlic cloves, minced

9 dried no-bake lasagna sheets, broken in half

3 cups tomato sauce

1 cup shredded mozzarella cheese

1 cup torn fresh basil

1. Preheat the oven to 400°F.

2. In a medium bowl, stir together the ricotta, tofu, oregano, red pepper flakes, and salt. Set aside.

3. Heat the olive oil in a 10-inch cast iron skillet over medium heat. Add the onion and sauté for 3 minutes. Add the zucchini and garlic and sauté for another 3 to 4 minutes. Remove this mixture from the pan and turn off the heat.

4. Into the skillet, place one-third of the zucchini mixture in an even layer, then drop one-third of the ricotta mixture in small spoonfuls on top. Arrange 3 broken lasagna sheets over the mixture and top with 1 cup of sauce, spreading well to fully coat the pasta. Repeat this sequence of zucchini, ricotta, noodles, and sauce two more times. Top the final sauce layer with the mozzarella.

⑤ Bake for 25 to 30 minutes until the cheese is bubbly and a knife is inserted easily into the noodles.

⑥ Remove from the oven, top with the basil, let cool, and divide into 6 squares. Into each of 6 containers, place 1 portion. Store in the refrigerator for up to 4 days.

Reheat Warm in the microwave for 1 to 2 minutes or in an aluminum foil–covered dish in the oven at 350°F for 10 minutes.

Freeze Freeze for up to 2 months. To thaw, refrigerate overnight and reheat in a 350°F oven for 15 minutes.

TIP A casserole dish will work in place of the cast iron pan.

Per Serving (1 square): Calories: 355; Fat: 14g; Protein: 17g; Total Carbs: 42g; Fiber: 5g; Sodium: 1214mg; Iron: 2mg

Caribbean Stuffed Sweet Potatoes

GLUTEN-FREE, NUT-FREE, VEGAN

PREP 15 minutes · **COOK** 1 hour · **MAKES** 6 servings

Sweet potatoes happen to be the perfect vehicle to pile on some Caribbean staples and flavors. The red beans pack a nutritional punch, with 8 grams of protein and 8 grams of fiber per cup. Slow cooker pork shoulder would also work well.

6 medium sweet potatoes

2 (15.5-ounce) cans low-sodium red kidney beans, drained and rinsed

1 cup water

1 tablespoon jerk seasoning mix

2 tablespoons avocado oil

2 yellow bell peppers, cut into ½-inch strips

2 red bell peppers, cut into ½-inch strips

2 medium yellow onions, halved and cut into thin strips

2 teaspoons salt

1 large mango, peeled, pitted, and chopped

1 cup Green Mojo Sauce (page 144)

2 limes, quartered

1. Preheat the oven to 400°F.

2. Pierce each sweet potato several times with a fork. Set them on a sheet pan and bake for 30 to 40 minutes until tender when pierced with a fork. Cut a slit into the top of each potato and break them open slightly. Set aside to cool.

3. In a large sauce pot, heat the beans over medium heat. Add the water and jerk seasoning and simmer for 15 to 20 minutes until the beans have browned a bit and the liquid has thickened. Taste and adjust the seasoning to your liking. Set aside to cool.

4. Heat the avocado oil in a large skillet over medium heat. Add the bell peppers and onions and sauté for 10 to 15 minutes, until everything begins to soften. Add the salt, mix, and remove from the heat.

5. To assemble, take 1 sweet potato and stuff it with about ¾ cup of stewed beans, about ¼ cup of sautéed vegetables, a few spoonfuls of diced mango, and 2 tablespoons of Green Mojo Sauce. Place a lime wedge on the side. Repeat with the remaining potatoes.

6. Into each of 6 containers, place 1 stuffed sweet potato. Store in the refrigerator for up to 4 days.

 Reheat Warm in the microwave for 1 to 2 minutes.

Per Serving (1 container): Calories: 430; Fat: 18g; Protein: 10g; Total Carbs: 61g; Fiber: 11g; Sodium: 1279mg; Iron: 4mg

Angel Hair Pasta with Herb-Roasted Asparagus and Halibut

NUT-FREE

PREP 10 minutes · **MARINATE** 5 minutes · **COOK** 20 minutes · **MAKES** 4 servings

As a firm but flaky fish that has a mild and sweet flavor, halibut is a great fish for meal prep. It's also a great source of omega-3 fatty acids and magnesium. This sheet pan meal makes it a time-saving win.

½ cup extra-virgin olive oil

½ cup tightly packed chopped curly parsley

¼ cup freshly squeezed lemon juice

½ teaspoon dried dill

½ teaspoon coarse salt

1 pound halibut, cut into 4 pieces

1¼ pounds thin asparagus, cut into 2-inch pieces

2 cups cherry tomatoes

2 medium shallots, halved and sliced

8 ounces angel hair pasta, legume-based if desired

4 tablespoons freshly grated Parmesan cheese

1. Preheat the oven to 375°F.

2. In a large bowl, combine the olive oil, parsley, lemon juice, dill, and salt. Whisk to combine and transfer half of this marinade to a separate bowl.

3. Add the halibut pieces to the large bowl and toss to coat. Let sit for 5 minutes while you prepare the asparagus.

4. On a large baking sheet, combine the asparagus, tomatoes, and shallots and drizzle the reserved marinade over the vegetables. Nestle the marinated halibut between the vegetables.

5. Place the pan in the oven and cook for 15 minutes.

6. While the fish and vegetables are roasting, bring a large pot of water to a boil and cook the pasta according to the package instructions until al dente. Set aside.

7. After 15 minutes, adjust the oven to broil and place the baking sheet under the broiler for 2 to 3 minutes.

8. Into each of 4 containers, place 1 cup of cooked pasta, 1 piece of halibut, and equal portions of roasted vegetables, and top with 1 tablespoon of Parmesan. Store in the refrigerator for up to 3 days.

 Reheat Warm in the microwave for 1 to 2 minutes.

Per Serving (1 container): Calories: 665; Fat: 31g; Protein: 45g; Total Carbs: 54g; Fiber: 6g; Sodium: 404mg; Iron: 6mg

Chicken Satay with Spicy Almond Butter Carrots and Coconut Rice

DAIRY-FREE

PREP 10 minutes · **MARINATE** 20 minutes · **COOK** 45 minutes · **MAKES** 4 servings

Isn't it the best when a selective eating partner surprises you with a newfound food love? Carrots and almond butter may sound strange, but it has become a new favorite in our house, and I hope you will find it just as delicious as a meal prep side dish. Chicken satay usually requires hours to marinate, but even a quick soak in this Thai-inspired sauce provides plenty of flavor that comes through days later.

For the chicken

1½ pounds boneless, skinless chicken tenders

2 tablespoons fish sauce

2 tablespoons packed brown sugar

2 tablespoons freshly squeezed lime juice

1 tablespoon grated fresh ginger

2 garlic cloves, chopped

1 teaspoon lemongrass purée

1 teaspoon sriracha

For the carrots

4 large carrots, cut into ½-inch-thick coins

Nonstick olive oil cooking spray

1 red Thai chile pepper, seeded and thinly sliced

2 tablespoons creamy almond butter

1 lime, quartered

▶

1. Preheat the oven to 375°F.

2. In a large bowl, combine the chicken, fish sauce, brown sugar, lime juice, ginger, garlic, lemongrass, and sriracha. Toss to coat well and place in the refrigerator to marinate for 20 minutes.

3. While the chicken is marinating, prepare the carrots. On a large baking sheet, place the carrots and spray with a small amount of cooking spray. Roast in the oven for 35 minutes or until carrots are slightly browned. Remove them from the oven and transfer to a bowl. Toss the carrots with the red chile and almond butter to coat them evenly.

4. As the carrots roast, in a large sauce pot, combine the water, rice, coconut milk, and salt. Bring to a boil, cover, then reduce to a simmer. Cook the rice for 15 to 20 minutes or until all of the liquid is absorbed and the rice is no longer chewy or tough. Add more water and simmer for longer if needed. When done, set aside.

For the rice

1¼ cups water

1 cup jasmine rice

¾ cup coconut milk

¼ teaspoon salt

⑤ Remove the chicken from the refrigerator. Heat a large skillet over medium heat. Place the chicken in the skillet, discarding the marinade, and cook for 3 to 4 minutes per side or until an internal temperature of 165°F is reached.

⑥ Into each of 4 containers, place equal amounts of chicken, roasted carrots, and coconut rice, and add in 1 lime quarter to squeeze over everything when ready to eat.

⑦ Store the airtight containers in the refrigerator for up to 3 days.

🔥 **Reheat** Warm in the microwave for 1 to 2 minutes or in a 350°F oven until warmed through.

❄️ **Freeze** You can freeze the rice, once completely cooled, for up to 2 months.

TIP You can use brown rice instead of white jasmine rice, but note the cooking time will be longer, and you may need more cooking liquid.

Per Serving (1 container): Calories: 610; Fat: 22g; Protein: 48g; Total Carbs: 58g; Fiber: 6g; Sodium: 998mg; Iron: 4mg

Rosemary Chicken with Maple-Roasted Winter Squash

DAIRY-FREE, GLUTEN-FREE, NUT-FREE

PREP 15 minutes · **MARINATE** 30 minutes · **COOK** 40 minutes · **MAKES** 6 servings

The easiest meal prep formula in our house is often some combination of roasted protein and starchy veggie, which is exactly what you get here. Acorn squash is great because you don't even have to peel it. The skin becomes soft and buttery when roasted. Chicken thighs are a nice, hearty protein, but rosemary-roasted chickpeas would work equally well for a vegan version of this meal.

For the squash

1 (2½-pound) acorn squash, seeded, quartered lengthwise, and cut into ⅓-inch slices

2½ tablespoons maple syrup

2 tablespoons extra-virgin olive oil

1 teaspoon sweet paprika

½ teaspoon salt

For the chicken

4 garlic cloves, minced

2½ teaspoons dried rosemary

2 teaspoons maple syrup

1 teaspoon freshly ground black pepper

2 pounds boneless, skinless chicken thighs

1 teaspoon extra-virgin olive oil

⅓ cup shelled pumpkin seeds

6 cups mesclun mix

1. Preheat the oven to 375°F. Line two sheet pans with parchment paper.

2. In a large bowl, combine the squash, maple syrup, olive oil, paprika, and salt and toss to coat. Transfer the squash to the sheet pans and roast for 30 to 40 minutes until pierced easily with a fork, then remove from the oven and set aside to cool.

3. While the squash is roasting, in a large bowl, combine the garlic, rosemary, maple syrup, and pepper. Add the chicken, coat it well, then marinate in the refrigerator for 30 minutes.

4. In a large skillet, heat the olive oil over medium heat. Add the marinated chicken to the pan and sear for 4 to 5 minutes per side. Cook until an internal temperature of 165°F is reached. Remove the chicken from the skillet and set aside to cool.

⑤ Reduce the heat of the skillet to low and add the pumpkin seeds. Toast for 5 minutes, constantly stirring to avoid burning them. Remove the seeds from the pan.

⑥ Into each of 6 containers, place 1 cup of mesclun greens, 1 tablespoon of toasted pumpkin seeds, and equal amounts of roasted squash and chicken. Store the airtight containers in the refrigerator for up to 4 days.

Reheat Warm in the microwave for 1 to 2 minutes or in a 350°F oven until warmed through. Greens may be stored in a separate container and added to the warmed chicken and squash if you prefer.

TIP Use sautéed kale or stewed mustard greens rather than raw greens if you don't mind an extra cooking step.

Per Serving (1 container): Calories: 380; Fat: 15g; Protein: 35g; Total Carbs: 30g; Fiber: 4g; Sodium: 338mg; Iron: 6mg

Grilled Persian Kebabs over Cauliflower Rice and Israeli Couscous

DAIRY-FREE, NUT-FREE

PREP 7 minutes · **COOK** 20 minutes · **MAKES** 6 servings

If coming up with recipes or deciding what to eat is a challenge in your house, I recommend drawing inspiration from people and places in your life. These Persian kebabs are inspired by my mother-in-law, who makes them for summer barbecues. In fact, she makes so many, they're often frozen and enjoyed until Labor Day, which is how I knew they'd make a perfect meal prep! These kebabs can easily be cooked on a grill or in a cast iron skillet.

For the kebabs

⅔ pound ground beef

⅔ pound ground lamb

1 cup tightly packed finely chopped curly parsley

1 cup finely chopped yellow onion (about 1 medium onion)

½ cup plus 1 tablespoon panko bread crumbs

2 tablespoons tomato paste

1 teaspoon freshly ground black pepper

½ teaspoon salt

Nonstick olive oil cooking spray

For the couscous

2½ cups water

2 cups dried pearled couscous

1 tablespoon extra-virgin olive oil

▶

1. In a large bowl, combine the beef, lamb, parsley, onion, bread crumbs, tomato paste, pepper, and salt. Mix everything together until well incorporated. Using your hands, form the mixture into 2-inch-long cylinders or sausage shapes. You should be able to form 24 kebabs.

2. Heat your grill or cast iron skillet over medium heat. If using a skillet, add a light layer of cooking spray. Place a few kebabs onto the grill and cook for 3 to 4 minutes on each side. Repeat with the remaining kebabs until all are cooked.

3. To make the couscous, in a large sauce pot, bring the water to a boil. Add the couscous, stir, then bring back to a boil, and cover. Reduce to a simmer and let cook for 10 minutes or until all of the water has been absorbed.

6 cups premade fresh or frozen cauliflower rice

2 shallots, halved and thinly sliced

½ cup pomegranate seeds

¼ cup finely chopped parsley

Salt

Freshly ground black pepper

④ In a large skillet, heat the olive oil over medium heat. When the oil is shimmering, add the cauliflower rice and shallots. Cook for 3 to 4 minutes, stirring frequently. Add in the cooked couscous and cook for another minute. Remove from the heat and stir in the pomegranate seeds and parsley. Add salt and pepper to taste.

⑤ Into each of 6 containers, place 4 kebabs and equal portions of cauliflower and couscous mixture. Store the airtight containers in the refrigerator for up to 4 days.

🔥 **Reheat** Warm in the microwave for 1 to 2 minutes or in a 350°F oven until warmed through.

❄ **Freeze** The kebabs can be frozen by storing in a freezer-safe container or food storage bag for up to 2 months. To thaw, refrigerate overnight.

TIP Lamb is a great option for red meat. Forty percent of the fat in lean cuts of lamb is monounsaturated, which is the same as what's found in olive oil.

Per Serving (1 container): Calories: 360; Fat: 13g; Protein: 24g; Total Carbs: 30g; Fiber: 4g; Sodium: 338mg; Iron: 3mg

Lemon Arugula Pesto,
page 149

STAPLES AND SAUCES

All-Purpose Mediterranean Spice Blend

PREP 5 minutes · **MAKES** about ½ cup

Rather than opening up four or five different spice jars every time you make a recipe, try mixing together your most-used seasonings for an easy blend that's ready to go. This one highlights flavors of the Mediterranean, but this is a good tip for taco seasonings or Asian spice blends as well.

2 tablespoons plus
  2 teaspoons dried oregano

2 tablespoons plus
  2 teaspoons dried thyme

1 tablespoon plus
  1 teaspoon garlic powder

1 tablespoon plus
  1 teaspoon dried rosemary

1 tablespoon salt

1. In a small bowl or sealable jar, combine the oregano, thyme, garlic powder, rosemary, and salt and mix well.

2. Store in an airtight container in the pantry for up to 1 year.

Per Serving (1 teaspoon): Calories: 5; Fat: 0g; Protein: 0g; Total Carbs: 1g; Fiber: 1g; Sodium: 291mg; Iron: 1mg

Dijon Tahini Dressing

GLUTEN-FREE, NUT-FREE, VEGAN

PREP 5 minutes · **MAKES** about 1 cup

Store-bought salad dressings can have a fair amount of unwanted sugar, salt, and preservatives, so having a go-to salad dressing recipe can make meal prep all the more healthy and delicious. Tahini, rich in heart-healthy omega-3 and omega-6 fatty acids, lends a creamy quality to any dressing base.

⅔ cup tahini

3 tablespoons freshly squeezed lemon juice

2 teaspoons Dijon mustard

1 tablespoon maple syrup

Water, for thinning

Pinch sea salt

1. In a small bowl, whisk together the tahini, lemon juice, Dijon mustard, and maple syrup. Slowly add cold water until creamy. The mixture may thicken at first, but continue adding water a little at a time and whisking until the mixture is creamy and smooth. Add the salt and adjust the flavor as needed.

2. Store in an airtight container in the refrigerator for up to 5 days.

TIP To reinvigorate the dressing after storage, give it a good whisk, heat for 30 seconds, or add a touch more cold water to loosen it up.

Per Serving (2 tablespoons): Calories: 128; Fat: 11g; Protein: 4g; Total Carbs: 6g; Fiber: 2g; Sodium: 70mg; Iron: 2mg

Green Mojo Sauce

GLUTEN-FREE, NUT-FREE, VEGAN

PREP 10 minutes · **MAKES** about ½ cup

The name of this recipe is a bit redundant, as *mojo* actually means "sauce" in Spanish. The term originated in the Canary Islands of Spain, but now mojos are adapted to their location and use spices and ingredients of the local cuisine.

1 cup loosely packed fresh cilantro

½ cup loosely packed fresh parsley

¼ cup extra-virgin olive oil

Juice of 1 lime (roughly 1½ tablespoons)

1 jalapeño pepper, seeded and roughly chopped

1 garlic clove

½ teaspoon salt, plus more to taste

1. In a food processor or blender, combine the cilantro, parsley, olive oil, lime juice, jalapeño, garlic, and salt. Process on high for 30 seconds. Scrape down the sides of the bowl and continue processing until the sauce is smooth. Taste and adjust the seasonings to your liking.

2. Store in an airtight container in the refrigerator for up to 1 week.

❄ **Freeze** Store in a freezer-safe container or divide into ice cube trays to form cubes that can be kept in a resealable bag for 2 to 3 months. To thaw, refrigerate overnight.

TIP Use this green sauce for the Caribbean Stuffed Sweet Potatoes (page 132) or drizzle over grilled fish or steak.

Per Serving (2 tablespoons): Calories: 117; Fat: 13g; Protein: 1g; Total Carbs: 2g; Fiber: 1g; Sodium: 279mg; Iron: 1mg

Salsa Verde

GLUTEN-FREE, NUT-FREE, VEGAN

PREP 15 minutes • **COOK** 10 minutes • **MAKES** about 2 cups

Fresh salsa is a great way to take advantage of peak summer produce. This bright green version uses tomatillos, or Mexican green tomatoes. When choosing tomatillos, look for ones that are firm, green, and shiny and have their husk attached. If you can't find tomatillos at your grocery store, send your partner to a local farmers' market where they are sure to be bountiful in the summer and early fall.

12 medium tomatillos, husked, rinsed, and quartered

½ medium yellow onion, chopped

½ cup tightly packed fresh cilantro

1 garlic clove, peeled

1 jalapeño pepper, seeded and chopped

Juice of 1 small lime

1 teaspoon salt

① Preheat the broiler to high.

② Place the tomatillos on a baking sheet and broil for 5 to 6 minutes, until the skins start to blister. Remove the sheet, turn the tomatillos over, and broil for another 3 to 4 minutes.

③ Carefully transfer the tomatillos and their juices to a food processor. Add the onion, cilantro, garlic, jalapeño, lime juice, and salt. Pulse the mixture until mostly smooth. Adjust the salt and lime juice as desired.

④ Store in an airtight container for up to 1 week.

❄ **Freeze** Store in a freezer-safe container for up to 2 months. To thaw, refrigerate overnight.

TIP You can easily skip the roasting step and process the tomatillos raw.

Per Serving (½ cup): Calories: 44; Fat: 1g; Protein: 1g; Total Carbs: 9g; Fiber: 3g; Sodium: 586mg; Iron: 1mg

Chunky Tomato Sauce

GLUTEN-FREE, NUT-FREE, VEGAN

PREP 5 minutes · **COOK** 20 minutes · **MAKES** about 4 cups

When my husband and I took a pizza-making class, one of the best takeaways was how to make a simple, flavorful tomato sauce for anything from pizza to pasta. Jarred marinara sauces can have a hefty amount of salt and sugar added in, but making your own puts you in control. This chunky version is perfectly freezer friendly as well.

2 tablespoons extra-virgin olive oil

½ cup chopped yellow onion (about ½ a medium onion)

1 (28-ounce) can diced tomatoes

2 tablespoons tomato paste

2 garlic cloves, minced

1 teaspoon dried basil

½ teaspoon dried oregano

Salt

Freshly ground black pepper

1. In a medium sauce pot, heat the olive oil over medium heat and add the onion. Sauté for 3 minutes. Add the tomatoes and their juices, tomato paste, garlic, basil, and oregano. Stir to combine and let simmer for 15 minutes. Season with salt and pepper.

2. Store in an airtight container in the refrigerator for up to 2 weeks.

❄ **Freeze** Allow the sauce to completely cool, then store in a freezer-safe container for up to 3 months.

TIP Not only is having cans of diced, whole, and crushed tomatoes time and money saving, but by processing tomatoes, we get more available lycopene, an important antioxidant.

Per Serving (1 cup): Calories: 111; Fat: 8g; Protein: 2g; Total Carbs: 11g; Fiber: 3g; Sodium: 57mg; Iron: 1mg

Sun-Dried Tomato Tapenade

GLUTEN-FREE, NUT-FREE, VEGAN

PREP 5 minutes • MAKES about 1 cup

There's nothing like a fancy word such as *tapenade* to slyly introduce a new ingredient to a picky partner. Olives on their own may not be your favorite, but when combined with sweet sun-dried tomatoes and fresh herbs, this paste may have you singing a different tune.

½ cup pitted kalamata olives

½ cup oil-packed sun-dried tomatoes

¼ cup tightly packed fresh basil

¼ cup tightly packed fresh parsley

1. In a food processor, combine the olives, sun-dried tomatoes, basil, and parsley and pulse to mix. Scrape down the sides of the bowl and continue processing until a semi-smooth paste forms.

2. Store in an airtight container in the refrigerator for up to 1 week.

❄ **Freeze** Store in a freezer-safe container for up to 3 months. To thaw, refrigerate overnight.

TIP Try this tapenade on the Tuna Burger with Sun-Dried Tomato Tapenade (page 127), in your favorite sandwich, or over pasta.

Per Serving (1 tablespoon): Calories: 16; Fat: 1g; Protein: 0g; Total Carbs: 2g; Fiber: 0g; Sodium: 63mg; Iron: 0mg

Peanut Sauce for Everything

GLUTEN-FREE OPTION, VEGAN

PREP 5 minutes · **MAKES** about 1 cup

If you're nervous about how a new recipe will taste, throw a yummy sauce on it. You can use this basic peanut sauce on everything from noodles and chicken to grilled vegetables and tofu. Feel free to customize the spice and citrus levels to your liking.

¼ cup peanut butter

3 tablespoons water, plus more to thin

2 tablespoons soy sauce (or tamari for gluten-free)

2 teaspoons sesame oil

Juice of 1 lime

½ teaspoon sriracha

1. Into a blender, drop the peanut butter, water, soy sauce, sesame oil, lime juice, and sriracha. Process until smooth, adding additional water to thin to your desired consistency.

2. Store in an airtight container in the refrigerator for up to 3 days.

TIP For an allergy-friendly version, swap in almond or sun-flower seed butter.

Per Serving (¼ cup): Calories: 122; Fat: 10g; Protein: 5g; Total Carbs: 5g; Fiber: 1g; Sodium: 530mg; Iron: 2mg

Lemon Arugula Pesto

GLUTEN-FREE, VEGETARIAN

PREP 5 minutes • MAKES about 1 cup

Knowing how to build a pesto is a skill I feel all home cooks should master, and it's really not as difficult or involved as you may think. Pesto can be made with just about any ingredient. Follow the simple formula of greens, nuts, cheese, and extras (oils, vinegars, spices), and you can create a dozen unique sauce combinations.

2 cups fresh baby arugula

½ cup grated Parmesan cheese

3 tablespoons raw, unsalted walnuts

2 garlic cloves, chopped

½ teaspoon salt

½ cup plus 1 tablespoon extra-virgin olive oil

Juice of ½ lemon

1. In a food processor, combine the arugula, Parmesan, walnuts, garlic, and salt. Process on high for 30 seconds. Add the olive oil and lemon juice and continue to process on high, stopping as needed to scrape down the sides of the bowl, until the mixture is blended smooth.

2. Store in an airtight container in the refrigerator for up to 1 week.

❄ **Freeze** Pesto can be frozen in an airtight, freezer-safe container, or divided into ice cube trays to form cubes, for up to 1 month. To thaw, refrigerate overnight.

Per Serving (2 tablespoons): Calories: 157; Fat: 16g; Protein: 3g; Total Carbs: 1g; Fiber: 0g; Sodium: 215mg; Iron: 0mg

Blueberry Chia Jam

GLUTEN-FREE, NUT-FREE, VEGAN

COOK 10 minutes • **MAKES** about 2 cups

Are you ever overzealous in your seasonal fruit purchases? If you find that you've picked up too many berries to consume for snacks, try turning them into a quick chia seed jam. This version is much less sweet than traditional jarred jams and relies on the mighty chia seed, rather than pectin and sugar, to create that jelly texture. It's a breakfast and snack meal prep lifesaver.

3 cups fresh blueberries

1¾ tablespoons chia seeds

Maple syrup or honey (optional)

1. In a medium sauce pot, heat the blueberries over low heat. As the berries warm and start to release their juices, mash them up with the backside of a fork. Continue smashing until no chunks remain.

2. Remove the berries from the heat and stir in the chia seeds. Taste and add a small amount of maple syrup (if using).

3. Transfer to a small glass jar and store in the refrigerator. The jam will continue to thicken over the next few days.

4. Store in an airtight container in the refrigerator for up to 2 weeks.

❄ **Freeze** Store in a freezer-safe container for up to 3 months. To thaw, refrigerate overnight.

Per Serving (2 tablespoons): Calories: 24; Fat: 1g; Protein: 1g; Total Carbs: 5g; Fiber: 1g; Sodium: 0mg; Iron: 1mg

Barbecue Roasted Chickpeas, page 159

SNACKS

Banana Sushi

VEGAN

PREP 10 minutes · **MAKES** 4 servings

Sushi isn't just for fish anymore. Grab your partner and make these peanut butter and banana roll ups for a quick and tasty snack. By cutting them into rounds à la sushi, you and your partner can each decide what portion you need in the moment.

Per sushi roll *(x4)*

1 whole-wheat tortilla

2 tablespoons peanut butter

1 tablespoon mini dark chocolate chips or cacao nibs

1 small banana

1. Lay 1 tortilla on a cutting board. Spread 2 tablespoons of peanut butter evenly over the tortilla and sprinkle this layer with the chocolate chips. Lay the banana close to one of the edges of the tortilla and then roll it up into the tortilla. Use a bit of extra peanut butter to create a seal, then cut into ½-inch pieces à la sushi.

2. Repeat with the remaining 3 tortillas and bananas.

3. Store in airtight containers, sandwich bags, or eco-friendly food wraps in the refrigerator for up to 3 days.

TIP Substitute a different nut or seed butter if there is a peanut butter allergy in your household.

Per Serving (1 sushi roll): Calories: 402; Fat: 21g; Protein: 12g; Total Carbs: 47g; Fiber: 7g; Sodium: 262mg; Iron: 3mg

Cucumber Caprese Snack Boxes

GLUTEN-FREE, VEGETARIAN

PREP 15 minutes • **MAKES** 4 servings

Not having to actually cook or do much prep is what snacking is all about. These Italian-themed snack boxes are full of antioxidants, fiber, and healthy fats. This concept can easily be repeated and reinvented a dozen different ways to accommodate changing taste preferences and to keep nutritious foods from becoming boring or bland.

Per snack box (x4)

¼ cup cherry tomatoes

½ medium Kirby cucumber, halved lengthwise and cut into ½-inch bites

¼ cup fresh mozzarella pearls

¼ cup pitted kalamata olives

Red pepper flakes

Dried basil

1. In a small container, combine the tomatoes, cucumber, mozzarella, and olives. Add red pepper flakes and basil to taste.

2. Repeat to make 3 more snack boxes.

3. Store the airtight containers in the refrigerator for up to 4 days.

TIP If you have leftover fresh basil from another recipe, feel free to use torn leaves rather than the dried herb for a more authentic caprese.

Per Serving (1 snack box): Calories: 139; Fat: 9g; Protein: 7g; Total Carbs: 10g; Fiber: 2g; Sodium: 383mg; Iron: 2mg

Mexican Street Snack

GLUTEN-FREE, NUT-FREE, VEGAN

PREP 15 minutes · **MAKES** 6 servings

Snacking on fruit may not always be the most exciting for you or a partner as you are learning to eat healthier, so let's spice things up. Street-side fruit vendors in Mexico sell mango on a stick with chili and lime, and this recipe pays homage to that flavorful snack. Jicama, or Mexican turnip, provides a crunchy contrast and is notably high in inulin, a fiber that helps with constipation and a healthy gut microbiome.

1 medium jicama (about 1 pound), peeled and cut into ½-by-3-inch-long matchsticks

Juice of 1 lime

1 teaspoon chili powder

Pinch salt

2 medium mangos, cut into ¼-inch wedges

1. In a medium bowl, combine the jicama, lime juice, chili powder, and salt. Toss to coat well.

2. Store the seasoned jicama and mango wedges together in an airtight container in the refrigerator for up to 4 days.

TIP The seasonings in this recipe can be replaced with Tajín, a popular seasoning mix of chili, lime, and salt. You can find it in most grocery stores or online.

Per Serving (1 portion): Calories: 112; Fat: 1g; Protein: 2g; Total Carbs: 27g; Fiber: 7g; Sodium: 37mg; Iron: 1mg

Pumpkin Yogurt Dip

GLUTEN-FREE, NUT-FREE, VEGETARIAN

PREP 10 minutes · **MAKES** 3 cups

Is your other half not so skilled in the kitchen? Well if they can hold a spoon, they can help prep this easy snack recipe. This autumn-inspired dip packs in protein and calcium from the yogurt and plenty of vitamin A and fiber from the pumpkin purée. Serve this with apple or pear slices (stored precut in the refrigerator in a tightly sealed bag to prevent browning), pretzels, or cinnamon graham crackers.

2 cups plain Greek yogurt

1 cup canned pumpkin purée

1 tablespoon maple syrup

1 teaspoon ground cinnamon

½ teaspoon ground nutmeg

½ teaspoon ground ginger

1. In a medium bowl, combine the Greek yogurt, pumpkin purée, maple syrup, cinnamon, nutmeg, and ginger. Stir to combine well. Taste and adjust the seasonings if desired.

2. Store in an airtight container in the refrigerator for up to 1 week.

TIP Make a large quantity of this pumpkin spice blend to have on hand for everything from muffins to lattes in the fall and winter months.

Per Serving (½ cup): Calories: 52; Fat: 0g; Protein: 6g; Total Carbs: 8g; Fiber: 1g; Sodium: 22mg; Iron: 1mg

Nut Butter–Stuffed Dates

GLUTEN-FREE, VEGAN

PREP 10 minutes • **MAKES** 6 servings

Dates are the perfect snack vehicle. This energy-dense fruit has even more potassium than bananas, and when combined with protein-rich nut butter, it keeps hunger at bay and satisfies a sweet tooth. You and your partner can easily customize the fun toppings to your liking, too.

12 medjool dates

12 teaspoons nut butter (almond, peanut, or cashew)

Ground cinnamon, for garnish (optional)

Unsweetened coconut flakes, for garnish (optional)

Flaky sea salt, for garnish (optional)

Crushed nuts, for garnish (optional)

① Use a knife to make a small slit into each date and carefully remove the pits.

② Spoon 1 teaspoon of your desired nut butter into the opening of each date.

③ Sprinkle with the optional toppings.

④ Store in an airtight container for up to 3 to 4 days.

❄ **Freeze** Lay the dates flat on a baking sheet and freeze until the nut butter appears set, about 1 hour. Transfer to a plastic or eco-friendly sandwich bag and store for up to 3 weeks. Eat straight from the freezer or let thaw to room temperature.

Per Serving (2 dates): Calories: 184; Fat: 6g; Protein: 3g; Total Carbs: 31g; Fiber: 4g; Sodium: 50mg; Iron: 1mg

Barbecue Roasted Chickpeas

GLUTEN-FREE, NUT-FREE, VEGAN

PREP 5 minutes · **COOK** 50 minutes · **MAKES** 4 cups

Protein-based snacks that are nonperishable can be hard to come by; yogurt, cheese, and meats don't travel particularly well. Roasted chickpeas, however, are perfectly portable and poppable snacks that are high in plant protein, potassium, folate, and fiber. If you're looking for more ways to add legumes to your or your partner's diet, these barbecue seasoned beans might do the trick.

2 (15.5-ounce) cans low-sodium chickpeas, drained, rinsed, and dried

2 tablespoons extra-virgin olive oil

1 teaspoon ground cumin

1 teaspoon garlic powder

1 teaspoon brown sugar

½ teaspoons sweet paprika

½ teaspoon chili powder

½ teaspoon salt

1. Preheat the oven to 400°F.

2. In a large bowl, combine the chickpeas, olive oil, cumin, garlic powder, brown sugar, paprika, chili powder, and salt. Gently toss the mixture to coat the chickpeas well.

3. Transfer the mixture to a baking sheet lined with parchment paper and roast in the oven for 40 to 50 minutes. Every 10 minutes, give the pan a shake to prevent the chickpeas burning. The chickpeas are done when they are lightly browned and the texture is more crisp than soft.

4. Store in an airtight container or food storage bag in the pantry for up to 5 days.

TIP The flavor combinations for these roasted chickpeas are endless. Use curry for an Indian flair, dried rosemary and basil if you're feeling Italian, or za'atar to transport you to the Middle East.

Per Serving (1 cup): Calories: 355; Fat: 10g; Protein: 12g; Total Carbs: 56g; Fiber: 11g; Sodium: 1013mg; Iron: 4mg

Carrot Cranberry Flax Muffins

NUT-FREE, VEGAN

PREP 15 minutes · COOK 13 minutes · MAKES 12 muffins

Not only does smart meal prep for two mean making nutritious snacks for the week, but it can also mean freezing a half batch of these muffins to rescue a snack attack or breakfast in the future. You can feel good about having a muffin as your snack when they're packed with vitamin A–rich carrots and high-fiber whole-wheat flour and flax. The orange zest and cranberries round them out with just the right amount of pop and sweetness.

Butter, for greasing

1¾ cups whole-wheat flour, plus 1 teaspoon

1½ teaspoons baking powder

1 teaspoon ground cinnamon

½ teaspoon baking soda

½ teaspoon salt

½ teaspoon ground ginger

½ cup dried cranberries

2 cups grated carrots

1 tablespoon plus 2 teaspoons grated orange zest

½ cup maple syrup

⅓ cup melted coconut oil

⅔ cup dairy-free milk (almond, soy, oat)

2 tablespoons ground flaxseed

2 teaspoons apple cider vinegar

1 teaspoon vanilla extract

① Preheat the oven to 425°F. Grease a 12-cup muffin tin with butter or nonstick cooking spray or fill with liners.

② In a large bowl, whisk together 1¾ cups of flour, the baking powder, cinnamon, baking soda, salt, and ginger. In a separate small bowl, toss the cranberries with the remaining 1 teaspoon of flour so they don't stick together. Add the grated carrots, floured cranberries, and orange zest to the other ingredients and stir to combine.

③ In a medium bowl, whisk together the maple syrup and oil. Add the dairy-free milk, flaxseed, vinegar, and vanilla and mix well.

④ Pour the wet ingredients into the dry and mix until combined. Divide the batter evenly between the muffin cups. Bake the muffins for 13 minutes, or until the muffins are golden on top and a toothpick inserted into a muffin comes out clean.

⑤ Store in an airtight container in the pantry for 2 days, then move to the refrigerator and store for up to 5 days.

❄ **Freeze** Store in freezer-safe containers or a food storage bag for up to 2 months. To thaw, warm in the microwave for 1 to 2 minutes.

Per Serving (1 muffin): Calories: 243; Fat: 17g; Protein: 3g; Total Carbs: 22g; Fiber: 4g; Sodium: 175mg; Iron: 1mg

Black Bean Hummus with Veggies

GLUTEN-FREE OPTION, NUT-FREE, VEGAN

PREP 10 minutes · **MAKES** 1½ cups

I never thought I'd get my husband to eat beans, but then came hummus. Sometimes it just takes introducing a food in a new way to open up someone's taste buds. Black beans are used in place of more traditional chickpeas, and the avocado lends an extra creamy element to this snack spread.

1 (15.5-ounce) can low-sodium black beans, drained and rinsed

½ avocado, peeled

¼ cup tahini

¼ cup freshly squeezed lemon juice

2 tablespoons soy sauce (or tamari for gluten-free)

1 teaspoon chopped fresh cilantro

1 teaspoon garlic powder

1 teaspoon onion powder

1 teaspoon chili powder

1 teaspoon ground cumin

1. In a food processor, combine the black beans, avocado, tahini, lemon juice, soy sauce, cilantro, garlic powder, onion powder, chili powder, and cumin. Blend for 1 to 2 minutes until the mixture becomes smooth and creamy.

2. Serve with the veggies of your choosing, such as carrots, celery, cucumber rounds, or bell pepper strips.

3. Store the hummus in an airtight container in the refrigerator for up to 5 days. Store the veggies in a separate storage container or bag in the refrigerator for up to 5 days.

TIP Some find that fresh beans (made from dried) result in a creamier hummus, so by all means, prepare a pot of dried black beans for this recipe instead.

Per Serving (¼ cup): Calories: 122; Fat: 8g; Protein: 5g; Total Carbs: 10g; Fiber: 4g; Sodium: 360mg; Iron: 3mg

Savory Granola Bars

GLUTEN-FREE, VEGAN

PREP 10 minutes · **CHILL** 1 hour · **MAKES** 14 servings

Grab-and-go snacks like granola bars are favorites of busy couples, but many people often question if these bars are really the best choice for them. My answer, as with many food items, is that if you can make it at home, you can be in charge of the ingredients and nutrition. These savory and slightly sweet bars take mere minutes to make and contain seeds and nuts that are high in magnesium, which can be beneficial for nerve functioning, bone health, and cell repair.

2 cups raw unsalted almonds, roughly chopped

1 cup shelled pumpkin seeds

1 cup rolled old-fashioned oats

½ cup brown rice syrup

½ cup dried cranberries

⅓ cup tahini

2 tablespoons sesame seeds (black or white)

1 teaspoon kosher salt

1 teaspoon dried rosemary

½ teaspoon dried thyme

¼ teaspoon freshly ground black pepper

1. In a large bowl, combine the almonds, pumpkin seeds, oats, brown rice syrup, cranberries, tahini, sesame seeds, salt, rosemary, thyme, and black pepper. Mix well until combined.

2. Line an 8-by-8-inch baking pan with parchment paper and pour the mixture into the pan. Using your hands, or something flat, such as a glass jar, press the mixture down firmly to form a well-packed layer. Refrigerate for at least 1 hour or freeze for 20 minutes.

3. Once set, remove the bars from the pan by lifting the edges of the parchment paper. Cut into 14 bars.

4. Store in an airtight container for up to 5 days. I prefer to store mine in the refrigerator to better maintain their structure.

❄ **Freeze** Wrap bars individually or lay them on a sheet pan to freeze before transferring to a 1-quart resealable bag, and store for up to 2 months.

TIP For a gluten-free household, be sure that your oats and brown rice syrup, which is often made with barley or malt for coloring, are certified gluten-free.

Per Serving (1 bar): Calories: 207; Fat: 12g; Protein: 6g; Total Carbs: 23g; Fiber: 3g; Sodium: 209mg; Iron: 2mg

Measurement Conversions

VOLUME EQUIVALENTS

	U.S. STANDARD	U.S. STANDARD (OUNCES)	METRIC (APPROXIMATE)
LIQUID	2 tablespoons	1 fl. oz.	30 mL
	¼ cup	2 fl. oz.	60 mL
	½ cup	4 fl. oz.	120 mL
	1 cup	8 fl. oz.	240 mL
	1½ cups	12 fl. oz.	355 mL
	2 cups or 1 pint	16 fl. oz.	475 mL
	4 cups or 1 quart	32 fl. oz.	1 L
	1 gallon	128 fl. oz.	4 L
DRY	⅛ teaspoon	–	0.5 mL
	¼ teaspoon	–	1 mL
	½ teaspoon	–	2 mL
	¾ teaspoon	–	4 mL
	1 teaspoon	–	5 mL
	1 tablespoon	–	15 mL
	¼ cup	–	59 mL
	⅓ cup	–	79 mL
	½ cup	–	118 mL
	⅔ cup	–	156 mL
	¾ cup	–	177 mL
	1 cup	–	235 mL
	2 cups or 1 pint	–	475 mL
	3 cups	–	700 mL
	4 cups or 1 quart	–	1 L
	½ gallon	–	2 L
	1 gallon	–	4 L

OVEN TEMPERATURES

FAHRENHEIT	CELSIUS (APPROXIMATE)
250°F	120°C
300°F	150°C
325°F	165°C
350°F	180°C
375°F	190°C
400°F	200°C
425°F	220°C
450°F	230°C

WEIGHT EQUIVALENTS

U.S. STANDARD	METRIC (APPROXIMATE)
½ ounce	15 g
1 ounce	30 g
2 ounces	60 g
4 ounces	115 g
8 ounces	225 g
12 ounces	340 g
16 ounces or 1 pound	455 g

Resources

General Information

→ **Casey Seiden Nutrition:** an online resource that features discussions on nutrition and living a healthy lifestyle, recipe inspiration, and tips for cooking for two and eating well together. *www.caseyseidennutrition.com*

→ **Fight Bac! Partnership for Food Safety Education:** an online resource dedicated to helping consumers prevent food poisoning. *www.fightbac.org*

→ **FoodSafety.gov:** an online resource for federal food safety information. *www.foodsafety.gov*

→ **The Original Intuitive Eating Pros:** a website created by authors Evelyn Tribole and Elyse Resch that offers resources for creating a healthy relationship with food, mind, and body. *www.intuitiveeating.org*

→ **United States Department of Agriculture:** an online resource for calorie calculators and counters. *www.nal.usda.gov/fnic/calculators-and-counters*

Supplies

→ **Amazon Fresh:** a grocery delivery and pickup service that is available as an add-on to Amazon Prime members. *www.amazon.com/amazonfresh*

→ **FreshDirect:** an online grocery store that delivers fresh products. *www.freshdirect.com*

→ **(re)zip:** reusable BPA-free storage bags and containers of all sizes. *https://rezip.com*

→ **Stasher Bags:** resealable silicone food storage bags that are heat- and microwave-safe. *www.stasherbag.com*

→ **Thrive Market:** a membership-based online retailer that offers natural and organic food products at a reduced cost. *www.thrivemarket.com*

References

Bauer, Brent A. "What Is BPA and What Are the Concerns about BPA?" *The Mayo Clinic.* Accessed June 1, 2019. https://www.mayoclinic.org/healthy-lifestyle /nutrition-and-healthy-eating/expert-answers/bpa/faq-20058331.

Hingle, Melanie D., Jayanthi Kandiah, and Annette Maggi. "Practice Paper of the Academy of Nutrition and Dietetics: Selecting Nutrient-Dense Foods for Good Health." *Journal of the Academy of Nutrition and Dietetics* 116, no. 9 (September 2016): 1473–1479. https://doi.org/10.1016/j.jand.2016.06.375.

"Storage Times for the Refrigerator and Freezer." *Fight Bac!* 2016. http://www.fightbac .org/wp-content/uploads/2016/04/PFSE-7696-chill-chart_FINAL.pdf.

U.S. Department of Agriculture. "Dietary Guidelines." *MyPlate.* Last modified September 5, 2018. https://www.choosemyplate.gov/dietary-guidelines.

U.S. Department of Health and Human Services and U.S. Department of Agriculture. *2015–2020 Dietary Guidelines for Americans,* 8th ed. Last modified December 2015. https://health.gov/dietaryguidelines/2015/guidelines/.

Index

Acknowledgments

I don't think "Thank you" is enough to encompass how grateful I feel for the support I received during the writing of this book. First and foremost, this book wouldn't have been possible without the support of my home "chef," my husband, Daniel. Thank you for always pushing me to grow and seize new opportunities, to be business savvy and creative, and to always stay true to my authentic message. I love cooking for you, having conversations about food with you, and wining and dining with you.

Thank you to all the members of my family—John, Kim, Zach, Karley, Anna, Tim, Carol, Michael, Lili, Matt, Eric, Julie, and Ellie—for allowing me to pick your brains, utilize your taste buds, and send you into the kitchen to come up with many recipes that have their roots in both of my families' histories. My fondest memories of food are related to family, and I cherish those times for where they have led me today. Thank you to my dietitian colleagues who advised me on this undertaking and for encouraging me to jump in with two feet. Thank you to friends who shared their excitement and knew I could write this book way before I even accepted an offer. Lastly, thank you to Callisto Media and the hardworking team it took to bring this exciting project to all the couples I'm excited to inspire.

About the Author

 Casey Seiden, MS, RD, CDN, CDE, is a registered dietitian nutritionist (RDN), and certified diabetes educator. She obtained a bachelor of science in food and nutrition science from the University of Vermont. She went on to complete a master's in nutrition and public health and her dietetic internship at Teachers College Columbia University. During her career in food and nutrition, Casey has worked with community nutrition programs and contributed her nutrition research and writing skills to national and international organizations and audiences. Casey is currently working in an outpatient setting providing bilingual medical nutrition therapy, counseling, and diabetes self-management training using an all-foods-fit approach to patients with diabetes and metabolic syndrome. She also serves as the current chair of the Steering and Envisioning Committee of the NYC Nutrition Education Network. Casey currently lives in New York City and can be found running miles around Central Park, visiting neighborhood coffee shops with her husband, or creating deliciously satisfying meals in her tiny apartment kitchen.

9 781641 527781